*f*P

The Scorpion's Tail

THE RELENTLESS RISE
OF ISLAMIC MILITANTS IN PAKISTAN—
AND HOW IT THREATENS AMERICA

ZAHID HUSSAIN

FREE PRESS
New York   London   Toronto   Sydney

FREE PRESS
A Division of Simon & Schuster, Inc.
1230 Avenue of the Americas
New York, NY 10020

First Free Press hardcover edition November 2010
FREE PRESS and colophon are trademarks of Simon & Schuster, Inc.

For information about special discounts for bulk purchases,
please contact Simon & Schuster Special Sales at 1-866-506-1949
or business@simonandschuster.com.

The Simon & Schuster Speakers Bureau can bring authors to your live event.
For more information or to book an event, contact the Simon & Schuster Speakers Bureau
at 1-866-248-3049 or visit our website at www.simonspeakers.com.

DESIGNED BY ERICH HOBBING

Manufactured in the United States of America

1   3   5   7   9   10   8   6   4   2

Library of Congress Cataloging-in-Publication Data
Hussain, Zahid, 1949–
The scorpion's tail / Zahid Hussain.
p.   cm.
Includes bibliographical references and index.
1. Pakistan—Politics and government—1988–   2. Islam and politics—Pakistan.
3. Islamic fundamentalism—Pakistan.   4. Terrorism—Religious aspects—Islam.   I. Title.
DS389.H878 2011
954.9105'3—dc22   2010026737

ISBN 978-1-4391-2025-5
ISBN 978-1-4391-5786-2 (ebook)

For Maria and Adnan

Contents

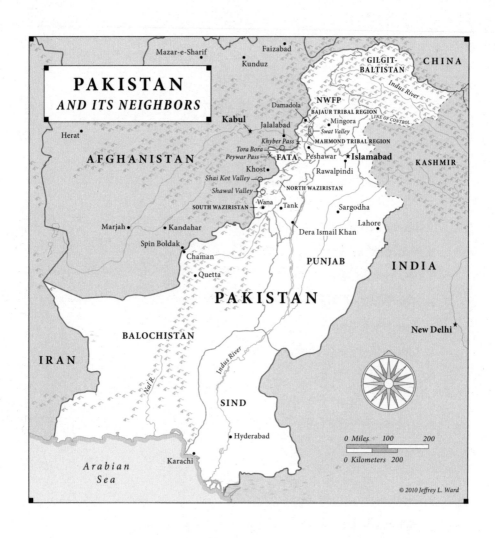

PAKISTAN
AND ITS NEIGHBORS

Mazar-e-Sharif
Faizabad
Kunduz
GILGIT-
BALTISTAN
CHINA
Indus River
Damadola
NWFP
BAJAUR TRIBAL REGION
Mingora
LINE OF CONTROL
Kabul
Jalalabad
Swat Valley
Herat
Khyber Pass
MAHMOND TRIBAL REGION
AFGHANISTAN
Tora Bora
Peywar Pass
FATA
Peshawar
Islamabad
KASHMIR
Khost
Rawalpindi
Shai Kot Valley
Shawal Valley
NORTH WAZIRISTAN
SOUTH WAZIRISTAN
Wana
Sargodha
Tank
Marjah
Kandahar
Dera Ismail Khan
Lahore
Spin Boldak
Chaman
PUNJAB
INDIA
Quetta
PAKISTAN
BALOCHISTAN
Nai R.
Indus River
New Delhi
IRAN
SIND
Hyderabad
0 Miles 100 200
0 Kilometers 200
Arabian Sea
Karachi

© 2010 Jeffrey L. Ward

The Scorpion's Tail

Introduction

On a hot August night in the remote town of Makin in Pakistan's South Waziristan tribal region, a short and stocky bearded man, hooked up to an intravenous drip, lay on a cot on the rooftop of a vast house. A young woman in her late teens massaged his legs. Nearby a Predator drone hovered in the clear sky, then zoomed in on the couple. Thousands of miles away, at CIA headquarters in Langley, Virginia, an operator sitting in front of a monitoring screen fired a Hellfire missile from the drone, killing the couple instantly. Only the man's torso was later found, the lower half of his body having been eviscerated. The young woman's body was shredded entirely.

The precision strike, carried out on August 5, 2009, killed Baitullah Mehsud, the leader of the Pakistani Taliban movement, and his young wife of less than a year. He was being treated that night for a kidney ailment. Baitullah was one of the most powerful of the radical Islamic militant commanders operating out of the remote tribal regions of Pakistan, on the border of Afghanistan. They had been launching a steady stream of attacks on the U.S. forces fighting in Afghanistan and had unleashed a wave of terror within Pakistan. Baitullah was blamed for the assassination of Benazir Bhutto in December 2007 and had claimed responsibility for a series of suicide attacks on Pakistani security forces and defense installations. His successor had also reportedly been involved in the planning of the suicide bombing of a remote CIA installation, Forward Operating Base Chapman, in Khost, Afghanistan, on December 30, 2009, that killed seven CIA officers. It was one of the worst attacks in history against U.S. intelligence officials.

Baitullah had declared that his ultimate aim was to attack New York and Washington. "It is a duty of every Muslim to wage jihad against the infidel forces of America and Britain," he said in 2007, in his first television interview, in which he appeared with his face covered. The failed Times Square bomber Faisal Shahzad said that he attempted the bombing in part as revenge for the killing of Baitullah as well as that of Abu Musab al-Zarqawi, the leader of al Qaeda in Iraq.[1]

The CIA was authorized by President Barack Obama to strike Baitullah immediately if it got a clear shot,[2] and as part of a dramatic escalation of drone surveillance in the tribal region, nine drones had been assigned to target him. The unmanned aerial vehicles known as Predator drones are able to track moving targets in real time, and their striking ability is extremely precise.

The Americans have been fighting Islamic militant groups waging an insurgency in Afghanistan and Pakistan since the beginning of the war in Afghanistan in October 2001. During most of that time the United States considered Baitullah a lesser threat than a number of other militant leaders. Most of his attacks were carried out inside Pakistan rather than against U.S. and NATO troops in Afghanistan, which was the focus of U.S. concern, and Washington had turned down repeated Pakistani requests to target him.[3] But the American position on him had changed as his power steadily grew and concerns mounted that escalating militant violence within Pakistan might destabilize the Pakistani government, throwing the region into even worse turmoil. Some suspected Baitullah's men of attacking the supply convoys for U.S. and NATO forces that traveled through Pakistan on the way to Afghanistan.

Two months before his death, in June 2009, Baitullah had narrowly escaped a strike when Hellfire missiles hit the funeral of an important Taliban leader who had been killed in an earlier strike. It turned out that Baitullah had left the funeral site only moments earlier.

The killing of Baitullah was perhaps the most successful strike in the eight-year history of drone operations in Pakistan. It was seen as a victory particularly for President Obama, who had ordered the escalation of the strikes in January 2009, shortly after his inauguration, as part of his overall review of the Afghan war strategy. Many other Taliban commanders and al Qaeda leaders have been killed by the strikes, most prominent among them three al Qaeda leaders—Abu Laith al-Libbi, Usama al-Kini, and Mustafa Abu al-Yazid—who were the masterminds of al Qaeda's terrorist attacks in Pakistan and Afghanistan.

The drone campaign has been hailed as a resounding success by some counterterrorism officials. On March 17, 2010, CIA director Leon Panetta described the raids as "the most aggressive operation that the CIA has been involved in in our history." He claimed that the campaign had thrown al Qaeda into complete disarray.[4] But others view the success of the campaign, and the larger success and wisdom of the current U.S. Af-Pak strategy, very differently.

The decision to step up the drone strikes was part of a growing recognition by the United States that the tribal territories in Pakistan have become, as Obama put it in his announcement of the new surge strategy in December 2009, the epicenter of the militant operations that have wreaked havoc both in Afghanistan and in Pakistan. Since the start of the war in Afghanistan, the remote tribal areas on Pakistan's border have become home to an ever more lethal stew of al Qaeda operatives, Uzbek militants, both Afghani and Pakistani Taliban, and local tribal militants. More than a dozen militant groups now operate from the territories, and the remote mountainous regions have become the main bases for the training of jihadists fighting on both sides of the Pakistan-Afghan border.

The number of militants now based in the region is believed to be between ten thousand and fifteen thousand. The largest group of fighters are associated with the Haqqani network, led by a legendary former Afghan Mujahideen commander, Jalaluddin Haqqani. With powerful influence on both sides of the border, the Haqqani network has reportedly been responsible for many spectacular attacks, including an assassination attempt against Afghan president Hamid Karzai in 2008, the kidnapping of *New York Times* reporter David Rhode, and the May 10, 2010, bombing of a NATO convoy in Kabul in which fifty-two people were injured and one Canadian and five American soldiers were killed.

In the first several years after the start of the Afghan war the militants based in Pakistan conducted attacks almost exclusively in Afghanistan, seeking to drive the U.S.-led coalition forces from the country and overthrow the Karzai government. Since 2007 they have also directed their wrath against the Pakistani military and security agencies, launching attacks of increasing sophistication and intensity, as well as perpetrating an escalating and more violent wave of suicide bombings against civilians in the major urban centers across Pakistan. A distinctive Pakistani Taliban movement has evolved, enforcing draconian Islamic rule not only in tribal areas but also in the neighboring North West Frontier Province. In April 2009 the Taliban forces extended their control still farther, taking over the Swat Valley, a popular tourist destination of green alpine meadows and snow-topped mountains, dubbed the Switzerland of Pakistan. The militants blew up scores of girls' schools, declaring female education un-Islamic, and executed hundreds of security and government officials. By late April they had advanced to within sixty miles of the Pakistani capital of Islamabad.

The Pakistani government and military, then both under the leadership of Pervez Musharraf, had been reluctant to launch major military operations against the militant groups, even in the face of heated pressure from Washington. In May 2009, however, confronting the harrowing prospect of the Taliban moving on Islamabad, Pakistani military finally launched a series of major offensives against the militant strongholds. Those operations have pushed the groups out of large portions of the territory they had claimed, but are still inconclusive. In some territories thought to have been cleared, militants have recently launched new attacks.

The militants have also infiltrated new terrain, far from the mountainous territories. They have turned the country's largest province, Punjab, into their new battlefield, launching a series of bloody suicide bombings and attacks on the urban centers of Lahore, Islamabad, and Rawalpindi, the headquarters of the army. Infiltrating deep into the major cities, the groups have divided into small terrorist cells, making them more difficult to track down. The port city of Karachi, a teeming metropolis of 18 million people in the far south on the Arabian Sea, has become a main hub of radicalism, offering the militants sanctuary as well as funding and a steady flood of new recruits from the thousands of madrassas spread across the city. It was in Karachi that Faisal Shahzad made contact with those who helped him make his way to the tribal territory of Waziristan for training in bomb making.

In the large southwestern province of Balochistan, the Afghani Taliban has gathered in and around the city of Quetta, near the Afghan border and the city of Kandahar, the spiritual capital of the Taliban regime when it ruled Afghanistan. U.S. officials believe that most of the Taliban leadership, including the spiritual leader of the movement, Mullah Mohammed Omar, are based in Quetta, though Pakistani officials continue to deny this. Scores of Afghan refugee camps were set up in Balochistan almost three decades ago, after the Soviet invasion of Afghanistan in 1979, and they have become centers of recruitment for the Taliban. The Quetta neighborhood of Pashtunabad looks like Kandahar did during the Taliban rule, with men in the Taliban's signature black turban openly roaming the congested bazaars and alleys. Local government officials estimate that Afghans now constitute almost 30 percent of Quetta's population of 1.7 million.

As the insurgency in Pakistan has escalated, it has grown not only in numbers but in sophistication, and the host of local tribal militant groups, which were once only loosely associated or even feuding, have formed an increasingly interconnected and coordinated web, with close collaboration between the al Qaeda and Taliban foreigners and the local militant leaders and Pakistani Taliban. Whether or not even the combined ground operations by Pakistani troops and the U.S. drone campaign can ultimately dislodge them from their strongholds in the remote regions and urban centers and defeat the insurgency is very much an open question. The operations against the militant groups have not only failed to stop the attacks, but have led to their dramatic escalation.

The drone strikes have been unquestionably effective in assassinating leading al Qaeda and other militant commanders and have greatly aided the Pakistani ground forces in their operations by helping to identify targets and militant positions. But they have also had serious blowback effects. The drone killings have stirred up a great deal of controversy in Pakistan, provoking intense anger among the Pakistani public and stoking heated anti-Americanism. This so-called secret war has become a focus of both militant rage and public protest. The United States has never officially acknowledged that it is launching the strikes, but they became public knowledge on January 1, 2003, when a drone crashed soon after taking off. For years Islamabad denied any knowledge of the strikes, fearful of public backlash, but the fact that the drone operations were carried out with the full knowledge and cooperation of the Pakistani government was widely understood by the Pakistani public. As the strikes have caused an increasing number of civilian deaths, including those of many women and children, public anger has surged.

The strikes have also spurred a significant rise in the number of recruits joining the militant groups, in part because according to tribal code, the families of the drones' victims are required to seek revenge. But recruitment has also risen among the youth of the well-educated middle class, who have flocked to the tribal regions from Pakistan's major urban centers. Baitullah Mehsud often boasted that each drone attack brought him three or four more suicide bombers.

Some counterinsurgency experts have wondered aloud whether the drones are doing more harm than good. "If we wind up killing a whole bunch of al Qaeda leaders and, at the same time, Pakistan implodes, that's not a victory for us," said David Kilcullen, a counterterrorism expert who played a key role in developing the surge strategy in Iraq. "It's possible the political cost of these attacks exceeds the tactical gains."[5]

For the first time in history an intelligence agency of one country has been using robots to target individuals for killing in another country with which it is not officially at war. No mention has ever been made publicly by either U.S. or Pakistani authorities of the collateral damage and its political cost. The leadership in Washington supports the drone program, and the Pakistani military and political leadership calculate that its effectiveness against the militants outweighs the danger of the rising public outrage. Off the record Pakistani military and government officials rave about its effectiveness.[6] Yet whether the drones can tip the balance in the fight against the insurgency is highly questionable.

The prime targets of the campaign, Osama bin Laden and the al Qaeda number two, Ayman al-Zawahiri, are still at large, and despite the loss of so many top leaders in the strikes, al Qaeda has grown in strength due to the new alliances it has made with Pakistani militants. Though recent assessments have asserted that al Qaeda has been crippled, and the number of al Qaeda forces operating out of Pakistan's tribal territories recently estimated at only one hundred, the truth is that there is a new generation of al Qaeda in Pakistan.[7] Comprised primarily of Pakistanis, it includes a flood of new recruits from the well-educated middle class, youth and professionals who have brought an increasing sophistication to al Qaeda's operations.

This new generation of al Qaeda is strongly committed to the cause of global jihad and has acted as a magnet for radicalized Muslims, including a number of Muslim American citizens who have traveled to Pakistan to receive training in al Qaeda camps for carrying out attacks within the United States. In addition to Faisal Shahzad, the Afghan-born Najibullah Zazi, who pled guilty in February 2010 to charges of planning to bomb the New York City subway system, traveled from the United States to camps run by al Qaeda in Pakistan for training. It is to be expected that additional such attempts will be made, and it may be only a matter of time before a serious attack is successfully carried out.

Militant leaders who are killed are quickly replaced; indeed Baitullah Mehsud's killing, hailed as such a pivotal victory, resulted in only a brief lull in attacks by the Pakistani Taliban. He was quickly succeeded by a fierce commander, Hakimullah Mehsud. Just months after Baitullah's death, the Pakistani Taliban took its wave of violence to a new level, launching a shocking series of highly coordinated suicide bombings and attacks in the major Pakistani cities of Lahore, Peshawar, and Kohat, targeting even high-security military installations. Clearly Baitullah's death had not hobbled Taliban operations in the least. The closely synchronized attacks exposed major weaknesses in Pakistan's security apparatus and demonstrated that the militants have become increasingly sophisticated in their planning and tactics.

The U.S. strategy for fighting the insurgencies in both Afghanistan and Pakistan is premised on rooting out the militants from territory after territory, steadily taking decisive control, while also weakening the groups' operations by assassinating their leadership. The United States now also seeks to train the Afghani armed forces and police to take over the fight in Afghanistan, and is working to gain the support of tribal leaders to renounce support for the militants. But the policy has thus far failed to make significant headway against the insurgency. Many experts argue that the war is now unwinnable.

In Pakistan even the major military offensives have resulted in only questionable gains, while stoking the fire of new recruitment to the groups and driving them into new strongholds in more formidable tribal territory—the most remote of the border regions, North Waziristan—and into the country's heartland.

A key flaw in the strategy for the fight against the insurgency is that it has failed to account for the ability of the groups to regenerate. As with the legend of the scorpion's venomous tail, which when cut off, grows back again, the militants have shown themselves capable of regrouping and striking back. The killing of their senior leaders has little effect on their operations.

The Pakistani military has now deployed 100,000 troops in the effort to root out the militants. Yet despite the increased deployment and ongoing drone strikes, militant attacks have resumed in some of the areas that were thought to be cleared. The threat represented by the insurgency has grown so severe that the stability of the Pakistani state is now seriously in question.

Relations between Pakistan and the United States are also strained. Mired in mutual mistrust, the two sides have substantial differences of opinion about the appropriate strategy in Afghanistan and how to deal with the wider insurgency. While Islamabad credits faulty U.S. policy with having pushed the war into Pakistan, with devastating fallout for the security of the state, American officials have often blamed Pakistan's ambivalence about cracking down on the militants in the tribal territories for the reversal in the war in Afghanistan. They have also accused elements within Pakistan's intelligence service and the Pakistani military of supporting some insurgent groups fighting in Afghanistan, including the powerful Haqqani network, to gain influence in Afghanistan, as well as supporting groups focused on fighting India. Pakistan denies all these accusations. The tensions have escalated as Pakistan has refused to launch a major offensive into North Waziristan to clamp down on the Haqqani network, which the United States sees as pivotal to its war strategy. The widespread perception among Pakistani officials and the military leadership is that the United States has no effective strategy for winning the war in Afghanistan. The Pakistani military has in fact begun pursuing avenues to a separate peace deal to be made directly with Afghanistan.

In June 2010 the war in Afghanistan became the longest war in U.S. history, and there is no clear end in sight. More than a thousand Americans have been killed and almost six thousand injured. When in December 2009 Barack Obama announced his strategy for the surge, he committed an additional thirty thousand troops to the war, almost doubling the number of U.S. soldiers deployed. The central premise of the surge was to seize the initiative from the Taliban, particularly in its stronghold in southern Afghanistan, and to turn over security responsibilities to the Afghan government, beginning withdrawal of U.S. forces by the summer of 2011. But the strategy has already badly floundered, and many Pakistani and American counterterrorism experts doubt that the military escalation can be a game changer by that time, or ever.

Marjah, a farming district in Helmand province, was supposed to be a showpiece of the counterinsurgency plan to clear areas of the Taliban and hand over control to the local governments. But many months after the February launch of the operation, involving some fifteen thousand NATO and Afghan national forces, the hold on the area is still tentative. The Taliban have melted back into the population and have been assassinating tribal leaders who have collaborated with the coalition forces. In May 2010 Gen. Stanley McChrystal, who was then the commander of the NATO forces in Afghanistan, called Marjah a "bleeding ulcer."[8] The remark was a pointed update of Soviet president Mikhail Gorbachev's characterization of the Soviet war in Afghanistan as a "bleeding wound." "Contrary to President Obama's promise that the deployment would disrupt, dismantle and defeat the Taliban insurgents and their al Qaeda allies, the insurgency has become more resilient, multi-structured and deadly," says a report by the Afghanistan Rights Monitor. The Obama administration now faces a situation as difficult as that confronted by the former Soviet Union at the end of its occupation of Afghanistan.

The implications for Pakistan of further military escalation in Afghanistan could be severe. Intensified fighting in Afghanistan and expansion of drone strikes in the Pakistani tribal areas and beyond are likely to further escalate the insurgency in the country. What is widely perceived as a rapidly diminishing U.S. commitment to the war has also intensified the country's long-standing struggle with India for supremacy of influence in Afghanistan. India has been aggressively establishing political and economic influence in Afghanistan, providing reconstruction assistance amounting to an estimated $1 billion, and the Pakistani military establishment views the expanding Indian presence as a serious threat to their own country's security. It is for this reason that the Pakistani military and the Inter-Services Intelligence Agency continue patronizing Afghan Taliban insurgent groups such as the Haqqani network, considering them vital tools for countering Indian influence, even at the risk of Islamabad's strategic relationship with Washington.

What has not been well enough understood is that the fundamental flaw in the U.S. approach to the war has been a failure to appreciate the extent to which this is not only an Afghan war, or only a war against Islamic extremists, but also a Pashtun war. It is ethnic Pashtuns on both sides of the Af-Pak border who have taken the lead in the insurgency. Both the Afghani and the Pakistani Taliban movements are predominantly Pashtun movements. They have been joined by several other militant groups and have formed a close alliance with al Qaeda, but they draw their fighters primarily from Pashtun tribesmen, who inhabit both sides of the border. These are the same tribal people who fought the Soviet Army two decades ago, and they will not give up this fight any more readily.

Establishing any kind of lasting peace in the region, and turning the tide of anti-Americanism and stanching the flow of jihadist attackers to the United States, will require not only military operations, but a political accommodation that takes into account the longer-term political and economic struggles in Afghanistan and Pakistan and the tortured history by which the insurgency has become so deeply rooted. That is a story that begins with the welcoming into Pakistan's remote tribal regions of a flood of Islamic radicals to fight the "Godless communists" after the Soviet invasion of Afghanistan.

CHAPTER 1

Witches' Brew

The densely forested, snow-covered ridge at 9,000 feet was home to the last Pakistani border post on the Pakistan-Afghan border, called Manrota. This remote corner of the Shawal Valley was thought to have once been Osama bin Laden's lair. When I visited there in February 2007 a faded green Pakistani flag fluttered on top of a mud compound that marked the Durand Line, separating the two countries.

"It is very difficult to keep a watch on cross-border movements when the visibility is less than fifty meters," said Major Faisal, a young battalion commander. We walked in single file to avoid land mines. There was no habitation for miles. "Down there is an American post," he said, pointing his baton toward a hazy structure hidden among thick pine trees on the Afghan side.

The Shawal Valley boasts some of Pakistan's most forbidding terrain. It is so remote that the Pakistani Army had never set foot there until U.S. forces arrived on the Afghan side of the border at the end of 2001. Tribal groups had ruled the area without interference for generations, and fugitives of many types had long found sanctuary there. The thick forests and natural hideouts in the many caves that dot the mountains made tracking down insurgents nearly impossible for

Pakistani troops. Across the border the Afghan Shawal, with its narrow valleys and high mountains, also presented a massive military problem for the United States. There was no way either U.S. or Pakistani troops could enter the valley in any numbers, as they would be easily trapped.

The Shawal Valley, which runs through the territory known as Waziristan, on Pakistan's northwest border, is inhabited by the Pashtuns, who have a long history of defiance against the government and have never capitulated to intruders. Divided into numerous tribes and subtribes, they are a strongly traditional people and fiercely protective of their independence. The Taliban movement that seized power in Afghanistan in 1996 was a predominantly Pashtun movement, with roots on both sides of the Durand Line. The remoteness of the territory, its history of relative autonomy from the Pakistani government, and its dominance by Pashtuns all made it fertile ground for the nexus of militant groups that has taken such deep root there.

Waziristan, which is divided into South and North, is among the seven semi-autonomous tribal areas of Pakistan known as the Federally Administered Tribal Agencies (FATA) that border Afghanistan. Under British colonial rule the policy for governing the tribal region was based on a mix of persuasion, pressure, and regular armed intervention. Britain stationed troops in FATA, but it also largely granted autonomy to the territories. That special status for FATA was regulated by a number of treaties that required tribal elders, known as *maliks*, to guarantee peace and keep open the routes for trade and troop movements between Afghanistan and Pakistan, in return for financial payments. After Pakistan achieved independence it withdrew its forces from FATA, but it retained the colonial administrative and legal structure. FATA formally became a part of Pakistan, but it more closely resembled a colony, its tribespeople deprived of many civil and political rights. Until 1997 the tribal areas did not have the adult franchise, only a small number of maliks were granted voting rights, and political parties were banned from operating in the area. That ambiguous status has largely been responsible for its economic backwardness and lawlessness.

Islamic radicalism first took root in the territories during the Afghan war against the Soviets in the 1980s, when the Pakistani government, in collaboration with the U.S. Central Intelligence Agency, pursued a deliberate policy of sponsoring Islamic militancy in the region as a tool of influence in the war.

The Afghan resistance war started after the USSR sent its troops to Afghanistan to install a puppet government led by the Afghan communist leader Babrak Karmal. At midnight on December 24, 1979, Moscow mounted a massive airlift into Kabul of more than thirty thousand troops. The pro-Soviet People's Democratic Party of Afghanistan had seized power in April 1978 in a bloody coup, but factional fighting delayed its hold on power. Moscow justified the military intervention with the Brezhnev Doctrine, which stipulated that the Soviet Union had a "zone of responsibility" that obligated it to come to the assistance of any endangered fellow socialist country within that sphere.

The international response to the Soviet occupation of Afghanistan was sharp and swift. U.S. president Jimmy Carter, reassessing the strategic situation in the region in his State of the Union Address in January 1980, identified Pakistan as a "frontline State in the global struggle against communism." Setting aside the sanctions imposed on Islamabad for its nuclear program, the United States offered massive military and economic aid to Pakistan as the country became the conduit for U.S. assistance to the Mujahideen fighters in

Afghanistan opposing the Soviets. China, Britain, Saudi Arabia, and other Middle Eastern countries also joined in aiding the Afghan resistance.

The CIA and Pakistan's Inter-Services Intelligence Agency (ISI) then joined hands in conducting the largest covert operation in history, with Pakistan inviting fighters from across the Arab world to gather in its mountainous territories, which became the main training base for their operations across the border. They were drawn to the fight by anger over radical reforms that were introduced by the socialist government in Afghanistan, such as compulsory education for girls and the prohibition of many traditional practices, including forced marriages and the paying of a bride price. Islamists viewed those reforms as a blatant imposition of secular Western values and they were deeply resented, especially by the Pashtun tribespeople on both sides of the Af-Pak border, who joined the cause in droves. An estimated twenty thousand to thirty thousand fighters from roughly twenty Muslim countries joined the battle, famously including Osama bin Laden and Ayman al-Zawahiri, who together later founded al Qaeda.[1] For the United States, supporting the Mujahideen was a cost-effective strategy of opposing the Soviets and scoring an important victory in the cold war. For Pakistan, supporting the jihad served its geopolitical purposes well. The country had long vied with India for influence in Afghanistan, and the Pakistani military perceived an opportunity to install a pro-Pakistan Islamic government, tipping that balance.

The recruitment of fighters was controlled by Pakistan's intelligence agency, the ISI, and was funded by both the CIA and the Saudi intelligence agency, whose conservative Islamic regime had an interest in bringing another Islamic regime to power. The Saudi influence played an important role in deepening Islamic radicalism in the territories and undermining the power of the traditional tribal leaders. The Saudis funded the building of hundreds of madrassas in the region, run by the extremist Deobandi sect of Islam, which had its roots in opposing British colonial rule in India. The Deobandi clerics quickly usurped much of the power of the tribal elders, and an indigenous militancy began to take root.

The peak of the fighting took place from 1985 to 1986, when the Soviet forces launched their largest and most effective assaults on the Mujahideen supply lines, forcing them onto the defensive. But a sharp increase in military support from the United States and Saudi Arabia allowed the Mujahideen to regain the initiative. In 1986 the United States supplied the Mujahideen with FIM-92 Stinger ground-to-air missiles, which proved highly successful against the Soviet's helicopter gunships, and the tide of the war turned. This shift in the balance of power forced the new Soviet government of Mikhail Gorbachev to acknowledge that any further escalation of the war would be a misuse of Soviet political and military capital. Gorbachev ordered the troops' withdrawal. The war had claimed the lives of more than fifteen thousand Soviet soldiers and was a catalyst of the disintegration of the Soviet Union in 1990.

The Soviet troops began withdrawing on May 15, 1988, after Pakistan and Afghanistan signed a peace agreement known as the Geneva Accord, which was brokered by the United States and the USSR. But though the last Soviet soldier left Afghanistan on February 15, 1989, the war was far from over. The communist Afghan regime put up a tenacious fight to stay in power, and a massive operation by the rebel Mujahideen forces in the spring of 1989 to capture the eastern Afghan city of Jalalabad ended in a humiliating defeat, even though backed by U.S. and Pakistani money and munitions. The communist Afghan government resisted the Mujahideen onslaught for another three years, during which the only significant success for the Mujahideen was the capture of the eastern province of Khost, and that was after eleven years of siege.

It was not until the new Russian leader Boris Yelstin ended economic and military support for the communist government in April 1992 that the Afghan government finally collapsed. This ushered in the bloodiest phase of the civil war, as Mujahideen fighters from rival tribal groups fought for power. Ahmed Shah Massoud, a charismatic commander from the Tajik tribe, centered in northern Afghanistan, seized control of Kabul on April 30, 1992, having repulsed an attack by the forces loyal to a powerful Pashtun Mujahideen leader, Gulbuddin Hekmatyar, who had the backing of Pakistan. But the situation was far from stabilized. Hekmatyar's men stayed within artillery range and continuously fired barrages of rockets into the city, and Massoud was never able to establish firm control over the country.

Afghanistan's resistance movement had been born in chaos, it spread and triumphed chaotically, and it was not able to find a way to govern any differently. The country fragmented along ethnic and sectarian lines, and local warlords became all-powerful, unleashing a reign of terror. Thousands of people were killed and Kabul was largely destroyed by the internecine conflict. One of the most notorious incidents occurred in February 1993, when the forces loyal to Massoud and another Mujahideen commander, Abdul Raaul Sayyaf, both Sunni Muslim, massacred some seven hundred members of the Hazara Shia community.[2] The raping of women was also widespread. This mayhem was the inspiration for the Taliban movement.

In mid-1993 some three dozen former Mujahideen fighters met in the village of Kashke Nakud, near Kandahar, to voice their concern over the lawlessness and factional fighting. That meeting led to the birth of the Taliban Islamic movement. *Taliban* is a Pashto word, referring to students of a religious school, or madrassa, and those who had received madrassa education comprised the majority of the group in the initial period. But thousands of fighters of other Afghan Mujahideen groups joined the movement in a short time, making it the most formidable force in the war-ravaged country.

The movement was led by Mullah Mohammed Omar, a former Mujahideen commander and a Pashtun, and he and his largely Pashtun followers took it upon themselves to clean the country of corrupt warlords. A village mullah, Omar was relatively unknown in Afghanistan until then, though he was known to the Mujahideen as a crack marksman who had destroyed many Soviet tanks. He attributed his decision to organize the group to a dream in which Allah came to him in the shape of a man, asking him to lead the faithful. Reportedly he had also been infuriated when he heard about a Mujahideen commander killing a young boy after raping him, the kind of brutality that had become widespread as the factional fighting raged on.

Within two years of its inception, the movement had succeeded beyond anyone's imagination, taking control over most of the country. In 1996 the Taliban swept into Kabul, and Omar assumed the title of Amirul Momineen, or Commander of the Faithful. In an emotional ceremony in Kandahar, he appeared on a balcony above thousands of cheering Taliban, wrapped in a cloak said to belong to the Prophet Mohammad, which had not been removed from its Kandahar shrine in sixty years and had never been worn before. His title, Commander of the Faithful, was an ancient Islamic title that had not been adopted by any Muslim anywhere for nearly a thousand years. Mullah Omar had rarely met with non-Muslims, and there is only one known photo of him, taken when he was a young man. A Pakistani diplomat who met him several times described him as an extremely shy person who hardly ever talked to outsiders. His regime, though, was anything but retiring.

The Taliban imposed its own interpretation of Islamic Sharia rule. It banned female education and forbade women from stepping out of their home without being fully covered in an all-enveloping burka; men were required to wear long beards. Public execution of those who violated these laws became commonplace, and the regime became an international pariah. Though it had seized control of most of the country, many of the non-Pashtun former Mujahideen groups joined together in opposition under the banner of the Northern Alliance, led by Ahmed Shah Massoud, which maintained a hold on part of northern Afghanistan.

The rise of the Taliban movement owed much to the backing of the Pakistani government and Pakistani Islamic parties. Madrassas in the northern territories were closed down for months to allow students to fight alongside the Taliban. Dozens of ISI and Pakistani Army personnel were attached to the Taliban forces, providing them with tactical and professional support. Most of them had operated in Afghanistan during the anti-Soviet resistance and had close connections to various Afghan Mujahideen factions. The ISI operative posted in Kandahar also worked covertly to buy the loyalty of commanders opposing the Taliban. The role of the ISI increased tremendously after the Taliban seized Kabul in September 1996 and took control over the rest of the country.[3]

The rise of the Taliban in Afghanistan gave great impetus to the growing strength of the Pakistani militant groups, and they intensified their recruitment in both the Pashtun territories and in Punjab, Pakistan's largest and most populous province, particularly in its southern region, which was a stronghold of Islamic extremism. The rising power of armed, battle-hardened zealots in the territories was alarming to many of the locals, as some of the groups pressed for the establishment of Taliban-inspired Sharia rule, and fear spread of the Talibanization of Pakistan. But despite those fears, the militants continued to enjoy the support of the ISI, which now used the extensive intelligence and militant network it had built up to support a new jihad in Kashmir.

In 1989 long-simmering political discontent among Muslims in the Indian-controlled and disputed Himalayan state exploded into a popular uprising, which soon turned into an armed struggle. Thousands of Pakistanis and Kashmiris, many of them hardened by the war in Afghanistan, joined the guerrilla war against the Indian forces. Many militant groups, such as Harkat-ul-Mujahideen, Lashkar-e-Taiba, Harkat ul Jihad Islami, and Jaish-e-Mohammed, were deeply involved in the fighting in Kashmir; most of these fighters came from Punjab, which borders India, and the North West Frontier Province. This policy of using the Islamic militias as proxy fighters to represent Pakistan's regional interests was playing with fire.

Not only was the devotion to Islamic militancy in Pakistan's tribal regions greatly strengthened during the Taliban's rule, but so were relations between the Pakistani groups and al Qaeda. All the major Pakistani militant groups set up training camps in Afghanistan, in many cases with the cooperation of al Qaeda, which had by then developed strong relations with the Taliban.

When bin Laden first settled in Afghanistan, after being expelled from Sudan in 1996, the relations between him and Mullah Omar were far from cordial, as the Taliban and al Qaeda had very different aims and political and religious philosophies. Mullah Omar openly ridiculed bin Laden among his followers, often referring to him as "the donkey." The Taliban leader would often lament that he had inherited the Saudi militant and had to treat him as a guest and protect him according to Pashtun traditions. "He is like a chicken bone stuck in our throat," Mullah Omar told a senior Pakistani diplomat.[4]

Over the years, however, relations warmed as bin Laden provided the Taliban with financial support, on which it became increasingly reliant, as well as al Qaeda fighters, who were instrumental in extending control over the rest of Afghanistan. The association with bin Laden also resulted in a hardening of Mullah Omar's already conservative views. Some Taliban sources credited Omar's decision to blow up Afghanistan's ancient Buddhist statues in 2001 to the growing influence of bin Laden.

During Taliban rule more than ten thousand Pakistani militants were believed to have received military training in camps in Afghanistan, which were run jointly by Pakistani jihadi groups and al Qaeda.[5] The evidence of their close connection with al Qaeda emerged when several Pakistani militants were among those killed in a U.S. cruise missile attack in 1998 on an al Qaeda training camp in the Afghan province of Khost, which borders North Waziristan.

Relations between the United States and Pakistan became very strained during this time, as the Clinton administration grew increasingly concerned about Pakistan's nuclear program. Tension also mounted over the regime's support for the jihadis in Kashmir. President Bill Clinton threatened to put Pakistan on the list of nations supporting terrorism, and in early 2000 U.S. Assistant Secretary of State Karl Inderfurth told Pakistani leaders that the administration was particularly concerned about reputed links between the ISI and the militant group known as Harkat-ul-Mujahideen, which Washington believed was involved in the hijacking of an Indian Airlines plane in December 1999.[6] U.S. officials suspected that the hijacking was sponsored by the ISI, but President Musharraf rejected that allegation, and he denied that the Islamic militant groups fighting in Kashmir were working under the patronage of the ISI. He also said that he did not deem them to be terrorists.[7] During a short stopover in Islamabad in 2000, President Clinton refused to be photographed with Musharraf.

But the September 11 attacks on the United States the next year resulted in an abrupt turnaround in relations. President Musharraf perceived an opportunity to end Pakistan's isolation from the world community, and within hours of the terrorist attacks he threw his support behind the U.S. fight in Afghanistan. He also abandoned Pakistan's support for the Taliban government in Kabul and agreed to provide logistical support to the United States for its planned invasion of the country. The new alliance was to have immediate and profound effects on the relationship of the militant groups to the Pakistani state, as well as on growing dissent within the ranks of the military and on rising anti-Americanism across the country.

During the 1990s the jihadist movement in Pakistan was focused entirely on supporting the regional strategy of the Pakistani military establishment: to liberate Kashmir from India and install a Pashtun government in Afghanistan. This focus now changed dramatically. The militants saw Musharraf's decision to align with the United States as a betrayal. At the same time, a massive influx into the territories of al Qaeda and Taliban forces fleeing Afghanistan greatly increased the power of the militant groups.

Anticipating the U.S. invasion of Afghanistan in the wake of the 9/11 attacks, Osama bin Laden and his close aides planned to make Waziristan al Qaeda's future base, knowing it would be a safe haven. Bin Laden knew that the Pashtun tribesmen of the region would feel bound by the honor code they call

"Pashtun Wali," which requires that even an enemy who seeks shelter should be provided protection. He was also prepared to pay the impoverished tribesmen generously for providing their "guests" shelter. Osama's men distributed millions of rupees among the tribal elders in return for shelter, and the tribesmen enlisted by al Qaeda received up to $250 a month in salary, a huge amount in a poverty-stricken region with so little employment opportunity. The locals also received large payments for renting out their compounds to the fugitives.[8] Bin Laden also knew that the region had become a hub of extremism by then and that many of the local tribal leaders and much of the general population there were sympathetic to al Qaeda. A few months before the 9/11 attacks, during an interview with an Arab TV journalist, a close aide of Osama's hinted of their fleeing to Waziristan in the event of war in Afghanistan.[9]

The U.S. military launched major offensives in the hunt for bin Laden in the Tora Bora Mountains of Afghanistan in early December 2001. A cave complex in the mountains, ironically built with the assistance of the CIA in the 1980s, was suspected of being bin Laden's headquarters. Some intelligence reports and intercepted radio communications of bin Laden giving instructions to his men trapped in Tora Bora suggested early in the offensive that he was within striking range of the Americans. But with only thirteen hundred U.S. troops in Afghanistan at that time, spread over many miles of such formidable terrain, and hardly a third of them acclimated to the altitude, they could not cover all the possible escape routes.

To increase the odds of capturing bin Laden the U.S. military subcontracted the job of securing a key set of vantage points and escape routes out of Tora Bora to anti-Taliban Pashtun commanders. The Pakistani military also planned to join the operation, and President Musharraf spent some two weeks negotiating with the tribal elders to get them to agree to the deployment of troops on the border. But then an attack on the Indian Parliament on December 13, allegedly conducted by a Pakistani-based militant group, Jaish-e-Mohammed, brought India and Pakistan to the brink of a nuclear war, and Musharraf diverted the troops to the Indian border.

Tora Bora fell to U.S. troops on December 16, and a flood of al Qaeda and Taliban fugitives crossed into Waziristan without much resistance. Some Pakistani soldiers who were sympathetic to the militants' cause were said to have looked the other way or even to have facilitated their entry. In March 2002, when the United States launched a further offensive in the Shahi Kot Valley, Operation Anaconda, several hundred more militants fled into Waziristan, rebuilding their central command there, concentrated in the remote Shakai area of South Waziristan connected to the Shawal Valley.

Intelligence estimated that Osama brought three thousand Arab fighters with him, and thousands more militants of other nationalities, including Chechen and Uzbek fighters, also fled Afghanistan into the tribal regions.[10] Video footage of Osama and al Qaeda's number two man, Ayman al-Zawahiri, shown on the Arabic channel al Jazeera in September 2003, seemed to confirm speculation that they had found refuge in the territory, as the terrain captured on camera was similar to that of Waziristan. In such inaccessible terrain Osama could swim like a fish in the ocean.

The Bush administration applied intense pressure on Musharraf to crackdown on the militant groups accused of being involved in the attack on Indian parliament and go after bin Laden and his forces. "I think it is very important for President Musharraf to make a clear statement to the world that he intends to crack down on terror," President George W. Bush warned at the time. [11] Under the intense pressure Musharraf launched a vigorous hunt for al Qaeda fighters, working closely with the United States. The Pakistani security forces went hard after al Qaeda fugitives, capturing some five hundred operatives within a few months after the start of the war. Most of them were caught as they moved out of the tribal regions into urban areas.[12]

The first big catch came in March 2002, when Pakistani security agents, accompanied by FBI agents, seized Abu Zubaydah, the head of al Qaeda's overseas operation, in the central industrial city of Faisalabad. The raid was conducted after electronic surveillance by American agents detected satellite phone calls from Afghanistan. Months later, on the first anniversary of 9/11, a team of Pakistani security personnel and American agents captured Ramzi bin al Shibh, one of the alleged masterminds of the 9/11 attacks, in an apartment building in a middle-class neighborhood of Karachi. Six months later, in March 2003, the security forces arrested Khalid Sheikh Mohammed, another mastermind of the 9/11 attacks, in Rawalpindi.[13]

Musharraf received a ringing endorsement and a pledge of substantial additional aid from President Bush when he visited Washington in February 2002. "President Musharraf is a leader with great courage and vision. . . . I am proud to call him a friend,"[14] Bush said at a joint press conference with Musharraf at the White House. The vigor of Musharraf's moves against al Qaeda was indeed impressive, but the story was quite different when it came to the Pakistani militant groups.

Musharraf had also vowed to suppress all Islamic extremist groups challenging the authority of the state and to rein in radical madrassas. On January 12, 2002, he banned five Islamic militant groups, including the three most powerful jihadi organizations—Lashkar-e-Taiba, Jaish-e-Mohammed, and Harkat-ul-Mujahideen—and he declared that no

Pakistani-based organization would be allowed to indulge in terrorism in the name of religion. But Musharraf was not willing to completely sever Islamabad's connections with the militant forces, and the ban was not applied to groups operating in either Kashmir or the tribal areas.

Also, although some three thousand militants were arrested in a sweep after Musharraf's decision to ban the jihadi groups, they were freed shortly thereafter without being charged. He and the military believed that they would be able to drive a wedge between the Pakistani militants and the al Qaeda foreigners, but they failed to appreciate how firm a hold extremism had in the territories and how vehemently the militants and the wider Pashtun populace were opposed to his regime due to his alliance with the United States.

The U.S. invasion of Afghanistan triggered a massive political shift in the northwest territories. Radical Islamic parties in the region united under the banner of the Muttehida Majlis Amal (MMA, United Council for Action). It was the first time in Pakistan's history that squabbling religious groups representing different sects had joined together in this fashion. In the 2002 elections the MMA ran on the slogan "It is a war between Islam and the American infidel," which met with great enthusiasm among the Pashtuns, who believed their ethnic brethren on the other side of the border were being victimized by U.S. forces and the U.S.-supported administration in Kabul. The MMA leaders also openly expressed solidarity with Osama bin Laden and Mullah Omar.[15]

The alliance swept the polls in the North West Frontier Province (NWFP) and in the neighboring province of Balochistan, and with its seats in Parliament and growing power the MMA emerged as a formidable political force at the national level. The outlawed militant and sectarian groups played a significant role in the MMA's election campaign, and several militant commanders who had fought in Afghanistan and Kashmir were elected to the national and NWFP state assemblies.

The installation of conservative Islamic governments in the two border provinces was to have profound ramifications. The Islamists used their newfound political power to enforce rigid Islamic rule in the provinces. Besides pushing for the adoption of Sharia laws, the administrations pledged to end coeducation and close down movie theaters, which were considered to be Western-inspired violations of traditional norms and values. Schools were ordered to replace shirt-and-trouser uniforms with traditional Islamic wear, and Islamic texts were introduced into the school and college curricula. These policies strengthened the hand of extremists within the ruling alliance who opposed female education, and in 2003 thousands of Islamic zealots smashed billboards carrying pictures of female models in the nearby city of Peshawar, declaring them un-Islamic. Nongovernmental organizations working in the field of female education were particularly targeted by the mullahs, who accused them of spreading obscenity. Intellectuals and artists were ostracized and regularly attacked by zealots.[16]

The anger at Musharraf's alliance with the United States also drove a host of Pakistani tribal militant groups to join al Qaeda's fight. A major force behind the recruitment was the belief that the American military operation in Afghanistan was directed against Pashtuns, a view that was powerfully reinforced by the installation in power in Kabul of the Northern Alliance in October 2001. This must be understood as a pivotal cause of what has become the ever-widening Pashtun insurgency.

By allowing the Northern Alliance, which was dominated by Tajik, Uzbek, and Hazara minority ethnic groups, to take over the reins in Kabul, the United States unwittingly intensified long-standing ethnic animosities and incensed Pashtuns. The power of the Northern Alliance came at the expense of the Pashtun majority in Afghanistan, which was marginalized in the new power structure in Kabul. In propping up the new government, the United States alienated the predominantly Pashtun southern and eastern regions of Afghanistan, which had been Taliban strongholds, drove a wedge between the governments in Kabul and Islamabad, and provoked heated anti-Americanism in the tribal territories.

Musharraf had warned the United States not to allow the Alliance forces to enter Kabul before a broad-based Afghan national government was put in place. In a tense meeting between Musharraf and Bush in New York in October 2001, just days after the U.S. invasion of Afghanistan, Musharraf had pressed this point. "It took quite some time to break the ice," said Maleeha Lodhi, Pakistan's ambassador to the United States, who was present in the meeting. Musharraf stressed that the war should not be prolonged and that the Northern Alliance must not be allowed into Kabul before an interim administration was established, with the possible inclusion of a contingent of moderate Taliban leaders. He argued that Afghanis would more readily accept an interim government that included moderate elements within the Taliban and that the hardliners who were close to al Qaeda would thus be marginalized.

Bush agreed to Musharraf's suggestion not to encourage the Northern Alliance to take over Kabul. But as the two leaders stood up to give a joint press conference, they were informed that the Alliance forces had just entered the Afghan capital. Musharraf was visibly angered, becoming red in the face, and Bush appeared embarrassed.[17] In the haggling over the structure of the new government at a conference in Bonn in December 2001, the Pashtun Hamid Karzai emerged as chairman of the transitional administration that would govern the country until elections could be held. Yet he was widely perceived to be mere window dressing, while the Northern Alliance took over the most powerful sections of the government, controlling the all-important defense, interior, and foreign affairs posts.

With the turn of events in Kabul, the Musharraf government lost any leverage it might have had to convince the tribal groups in the territories to support the crackdown on al Qaeda and the Taliban.

Though some tribesmen did make an agreement with the Pakistani government in early 2002 to capture or evict foreign militants in their area in exchange for the building of roads and a new school, when the government delivered on its promises the tribal leaders failed to turn over any of the foreigners, denying that they had given them shelter. By the spring of 2002 U.S. intelligence and the Pakistani ISI reported that al Qaeda had regrouped in both South and North Waziristan, and the United States pressed Musharraf to launch a major military offensive against them. But the military was opposed and Musharraf soft-peddled, attempting instead to bring the groups around by negotiating peace deals with them.

Gen. Ali Muhammed Jan Orakzai, the commander of Pakistani forces in the area containing Waziristan, dismissed the reports of al Qaeda's resurgence. Although born in the tribal region, Orakzai had not served in the northwestern region before, and he had little understanding of the developments there after September 11. The general considered the American and ISI warnings about al Qaeda to be mere "guesswork," saying that his soldiers had "found nothing." [18] There was speculation that he deliberately ignored the large presence of foreigners because he feared that action against them would spark a tribal uprising.

The reality of the al Qaeda presence in the territories could no longer be denied, however, after the night of June 25, 2002, when several Pakistani Army commandos were killed in a clash with Arab fighters. The troops had surrounded a compound in Kazha Punga village in South Waziristan after reports of the presence of some key al Qaeda operatives there. The planned ambush turned into a disaster after some thirty-five militants escaped, killing ten commandos. Musharraf said the operation was a turning point "because it highlighted the magnitude of and seriousness of the threat."[19] The incident made clear that the foreign fighters had substantial local support and was a stark indication of the growing power of al Qaeda in Waziristan.

The Kazha Punga incident also convinced Musharraf of the need to create a fast-reacting force to counter the al Qaeda threat, but a number of problems hampered the Pakistani military's operations. A small number of U.S. Special Operations forces were allowed to accompany Pakistani forces on a number of raids in the tribal areas in 2002 and early 2003, and these raids were extremely controversial within the Pakistani military. Although Pakistani officials publicly denied the presence of Americans on these incursions, local tribesmen had no trouble spotting them and vigorously protested. The military feared that a full-scale tribal rebellion would break out, and under pressure from Musharraf, the Bush administration decided in 2003 to pull out its special forces from the territory. In recognition of the political risks that Musharraf had taken in allowing the U.S. forces into the territories, U.S. Deputy Secretary of State Richard Armitage said, "We were pushing them almost to the breaking point."[20]

The absence of any good ground intelligence and a lack of coordination between the army and the intelligence services also hampered the Pakistani military's operations, and the number of troops Musharraf was willing to dedicate to the hunt was limited by the perceived need to keep a large deployment on the country's border with India.

U.S. jets frequently bombed the suspected al Qaeda sanctuaries as American frustration with Pakistan's inability to rout al Qaeda from the territories grew. Musharraf warned tribal leaders that U.S. forces would be allowed to cross the Afghan border if the al Qaeda sanctuaries were not dismantled, but the local groups paid no heed.

By that time, however, the American focus had shifted decisively from Afghanistan to the launch of the war in Iraq, and the massive diversion of U.S. troops to the Iraqi theater cleared the way for the insurgency in Afghanistan. The Pakistani militant groups played an essential role in those operations. The fighting forces of a number of the tribal militant leaders had by now become quite formidable, and they were launching regular attacks against the U.S. forces as well as Afghani targets in Afghanistan.

One of the most powerful militant leaders was Hafiz Gul Bahadur, an Afghan civil war veteran and extremist cleric, who was based in North Waziristan. Closely associated with al Qaeda, he used his negotiating skills and personal charisma to build ties with many local tribesmen, building a strong foundation of support. He raised a fighting force of several thousand, who regularly staged attacks on the coalition forces in Afghanistan and launched a number of deadly attacks on the Pakistani Army.

Gul Bahadur, who was born in the small town of Madda Khel, close to the Afghanistan-Pakistan border, received his education in a local Deobandi madrassa and identified himself as a Hafiz, or one who has memorized the entire Quran. He first emerged on the scene months before the 9/11 attacks, when he threatened to attack monitors that the United Nations planned to deploy on the border region to halt the flow of weapons to the Taliban regime.[21] Vehemently opposed to the deployment of those monitors, he raised a militia of as many as four thousand volunteers, though in the end they were never deployed, due in part to the disruption created by the 9/11 attacks. He professed an unwavering commitment to holy war against the U.S.-led coalition forces in Afghanistan.[22]

The most enigmatic of the militant commanders, Gul Bahadur maintained a private profile and avoided interviews with journalists, which many of the other militant leaders were happy to give. He even banned journalists working for Western news agencies from operating in his territory, accusing them of having ties to foreign intelligence agencies, which he declared were "harmful for Islam, Muslims and the country." [23] Gul Bahadur strengthened his position by making alliances with a number of other clerics in the area, such as Maulana Sadiq Noor, another Afghan civil war veteran. That hard-line cleric ran a madrassa in Khati Keley, a village outside Miranshah, which hosted Arabs and Uzbek fighters, and he organized his own tribal militia after the government forces raided his seminary to flush out the foreign fighters.

Gul Bahadur signed a series of peace deals with the Pakistani government, which agreed to end all military operations against him in exchange for his expulsion of foreign fighters from the territory he controlled. But he never delivered on those promises, instead using the accords to create an umbrella of protection for al Qaeda forces. His fighters would battle with the Pakistani Army from time to time and also confront other militant groups, particularly Uzbeks, whom he perceived to be encroaching on his area of control. Maintaining his sphere of influence seemed to motivate Gul Bahadur more than any other factor, and he used his attacks on the military primarily as bargaining chips, never escalating to a degree that would risk a major operation against him. As a result, neither a firm truce with nor a complete defeat of Gul Bahadur seemed a likely prospect, and his limited raids were largely ignored by Pakistani forces.

North Waziristan had also become the home base of one of the most powerful Afghan militant leaders, Jalaluddin Haqqani, who wielded considerable influence on both sides of the Pakistan-Afghanistan border. A former anti-Soviet resistance commander, Haqqani was known for his ruthless effectiveness as a fighter. During the war against the Soviets he had also developed strong ties with the CIA and the ISI.[24]

It was 1989 when I first met Haqqani in the town of Miranshah, in North Waziristan, on the Afghan border. His forces were then fighting to liberate the town of Khost from Soviet occupation. He and his commanders were providing sanctuary to a top Afghan military commander, Gen. Shanawaz Tanai, after he defected from the Soviet-backed government. A stout man with a long, bushy beard, Haqqani could be distinguished by his huge turban. He was influenced particularly by the radical political Islamic views espoused by the Muslim Brotherhood, as were so many of the Mujahideen leaders at that time. Fluent in Arabic, he became close to bin Laden during the anti-Soviet war, and the relationship between the two strengthened during the Taliban's rule in Afghanistan, from 1996 to 2001. During this period he served as minister for the frontier region, and in late September 2001, just before the U.S. invasion of Afghanistan, Mullah Omar appointed Haqqani the commander in chief of the Taliban forces. After the ouster of the Taliban regime by the Americans he moved into North Waziristan and regrouped his militant force, launching regular attacks against the U.S.-led forces in eastern Afghanistan. Some believe he helped bin Laden escape the Tora Bora attacks.[25]

Haqqani wielded influence not only as a militant commander but as a spiritual leader. His family had established a number of madrassas in North Waziristan; the largest among them was 'Manba-e-Uloom (Source of knowledge), located just outside Miranshah. In 2002 Pakistani troops raided the complex, which also housed his family's residential quarters, after reports that it was being used by al Qaeda and the Taliban for their meetings, but did not manage to apprehend any significant militant leaders. It was the first time that U.S. officials had accompanied the Pakistani Army on a raid. When I toured the complex two days later the corridors of the sprawling madrassa were strewn with broken doors and pieces of glass. "American soldiers in Pakistani dress stood there watching the whole operation," said a member of the staff.[26] The madrassa was stormed many more times, but nothing significant was discovered in these raids.

After failing health forced Haqqani to go into semiretirement he appointed his eldest son, Sirajuddin, to take charge of the network and all of its operations with the Taliban in Afghanistan. In his late twenties, Sirajuddin immediately made his mark by extending his area of operation. He represented a new generation of Taliban commanders, who were more aggressive and more ruthless. He extended the network's activities in Afghanistan beyond Khost, Paktia, and Paktika provinces to the Ghazni, Logar, Wardak, and Kabul provinces and provided support to Taliban networks in Kunar, Nangarhar, Helmand, and Kandahar provinces. His force also drew many new recruits from among the militants in Pakistan, Uzbekistan, Chechnya, Turkey, and Middle Eastern countries.[27]

Sirajuddin quickly eclipsed his father in power and influence and rivaled more senior leaders for overall leadership of the Taliban. In many ways he was smarter and more respected than many of them, and strong connections he formed with top al Qaeda leaders made him the most dangerous militant commander not only in the territories but also in Afghanistan. Some senior Pakistani security officials believed that he wielded much greater influence in Afghanistan than even Mullah Omar. The U.S. Army also identified Sirajuddin as the primary threat to security in eastern Afghanistan.[28]

Under Sirajuddin the Haqqani network became increasingly violent and was responsible for more and more complex attacks inside Afghanistan. Sirajuddin claimed responsibility for a series of suicide attacks around Kabul and for the failed assassination attempt on President Hamid Karzai of Afghanistan at an Independence Day parade in the capital in 2002. "Yes, I organized those attacks," Sirajuddin later said, "but I had help from a serving Afghan military general." The United States placed a $200,000 bounty on his head.[29]

But despite increasing American pressure, Pakistani military authorities largely turned their backs on the activities of the Haqqani network. Western intelligence experts argue that the ISI has maintained links with Haqqani, considering him a strategic asset for maintaining a degree of influence in Afghanistan.[30] Pakistani military officials admitted at the time to having contact with the network but dismissed the allegation of aiding and abetting its activities. "Intelligence agencies worldwide maintain such contacts," said a senior ISI official.[31]

The Haqqanis were also important to the military due to their influence over the other tribal militants, particularly in North Waziristan, as so many of them had fought under Jalaluddin Haqqani's command in the fight against the Soviets. Islamabad believed that by dealing with the Haqqanis it could exercise influence over the other militant groups. Musharraf's preferred strategy for contending with their growing power was to negotiate, and the Haqqani family did help broker a number of peace deals with Gul Bahadur and other militant leaders. For these reasons, the military had no interest in a confrontation with the Haqqanis, which was to become a source of increasing tension between the United States and Pakistan as the insurgency escalated out of control.

Musharraf and his military leadership believed they could hunt down al Qaeda while also eventually reining in the militant groups that the government had formerly sponsored. There was also still considerable support within the military for the Taliban cause in Afghanistan, despite Musharraf's turnaround, and he was constrained in how vigorously the military was willing to crack down on the local militants' support for the insurgency. He was also reluctant to further alienate the groups, knowing that after the Americans left Afghanistan, the militants would once again be useful tools for exerting influence both in Afghanistan and in the continuing struggle in Kashmir.

Pakistan's reluctance to more vigorously clamp down on the rise of the tribal militants—which has now played such a powerful role in the failure of the Afghan war and also threatened to destabilize the Pakistani state—can not be fully understood without an appreciation of the longer history of the struggle between the forces of extremist Islam and the Pakistani state. That struggle has plagued the country since its birth, as has the struggle with India, and both played crucial roles in the rise of the insurgents.

CHAPTER 2

An Islamic State

More than six decades ago Pakistan was born as an independent state, carved out from the Indian subcontinent at the end of British rule in India, in August 1947. Comprising two swaths of predominantly Muslim territory, one much larger, in the northwest, and the other in the northeast, separated by thousands of miles, the country was established as a homeland for Muslims. Though Pakistan was not founded as an Islamic theocratic state, from the start a battle ensued between moderate Muslims, who championed a modern, democratic government, and Islamists, who agitated for a theocracy. Throughout its history Pakistan has been a state in search of its identity, and the struggle between Islamists and moderates has remained at the center of that quest.

This is in essence the same struggle currently playing out between the radical Islamists spearheading the insurgency and the Pakistani state, and understanding the longer history of this struggle is crucial to understanding why the Islamic militancy and extremism have gained such momentum, and why they were allowed to rage out of control. It is vital to understanding why the Pakistani state, and more particularly the military and the government, was so quick to welcome the jihadis into the northern territories in the fight against the

Soviets, and why the state then threw its support behind the Taliban. And it is vital to understanding why the Musharraf government was so reluctant to take decisive action against the Islamic extremist and militant groups.

Throughout the course of Pakistan's tortured history, the forces of radical Islam have succeeded in infusing religion into the very fabric of the state, into the political party system, and into the military and security services. Islamist parties, though never able to win a majority in Parliament, have secured far greater influence than the number of their supporters justifies, preventing the development of a sustainable liberal democracy in the country. Despite their majority in the Parliament the liberal and secular parties have not been able to overturn retrogressive laws regarding religious minorities and women's rights. Since its birth Pakistan has vacillated between periods of military rule and chaotic and corruption-riddled democratic regimes.

The infusion of radical Islamic ideology into the civil and military institutions has also been a major constraint on the fight against extremist militancy. It is this long legacy that accounts for the strong opposition President Musharraf faced from the military when he allied the country with the United States in the war in Afghanistan and that acted as a brake in launching operations against Pakistani militants in the territories.

Nothing can be understood about the current chaos in Pakistan, and about the prospects for ever bringing about an end to the insurgency, without appreciating the history of the long struggle over what would be the role of Islam in the Pakistani state.

The movement for the formation of Pakistan was led by Mohammed Ali Jinnah, a British-trained lawyer born to a wealthy family of businessmen in Karachi in 1876. He founded a political party, the Muslim League, which was a secular organization, trained in modern political methods, that represented the socioeconomic interests of the Muslim minority in India. Jinnah's vision for Pakistan was of a modern democratic state, and Islamic fundamentalists opposed his demand for a separate Muslim homeland and considered him a heretic. Major opposition to the push for Pakistani independence came from clerics of the Deobandi sect, which now has such a hold over the northern territories. The Deobandis had devoted years to the cause of freeing India from British colonial rule, and they rejected the idea of Pakistan as a British conspiracy. Their view was that the division of India would weaken the power of Muslims and undermine their objective of returning the entire subcontinent to Muslim rule.[1] When Partition did come it was an unprecedented upheaval, with millions of people slaughtered and an estimated 10 million to 15 million uprooted from their homes in the largest forced migration in history.

Ferocious fighting broke out between Hindus and Muslims; there was widespread looting, and thousands of women were killed after being raped. Many trains carrying refugees to Pakistan were blown up and their passengers slaughtered. A report in *Time* magazine on October 27, 1947, captured the horror vividly:

In the first six weeks of Independence, about half as many Indians were killed as Americans died during nearly four years of the second World War. There is still no possible numbering of the wounded and the mutilated who survived, or of those who must yet die for lack of the simplest medical facilities, or of so much as a roof over their heads. It is unbearable, and unwise as well, to cherish the memory of the bestial atrocities which have been perpetrated by Moslem and Sikh and Hindu alike. It is beyond human competence to conceive, far less to endure the thought of, the massiveness of the mania of rage, the munificence of the anguish, the fecundity of hate breeding hate, perhaps for generations to come.[2]

The bloodbath left the newly independent nations of India and Pakistan in a state of perpetual conflict. Many issues were left unresolved between the two countries, including the distribution of assets and the future of dozens of princely states, which became disputed territories. The most contentious was the predominantly Muslim state of Kashmir, in the Himalayan territory in the northern region between India and Pakistan. Just one year after Partition the two countries went to war over their rival claims to Kashmir; thousands of armed tribesmen from Waziristan and other areas of northwestern Pakistan invaded the territory. Pakistan now controls one third of Kashmir and India governs the rest, but those boundary lines are still hotly disputed and the conflict has continued to rage, flaring up into two more wars and to the brink of war on several occasions over the past sixty years.

The conflict over Kashmir has been a major determinant of Pakistan's security and foreign policy, serving almost as the raison d'être for Pakistan's existence. This conflict and the perceived threat of being dominated by its more powerful neighbor have been instrumental in Islamabad's use of Islamic militancy as a foreign policy tool and lies behind its intense interest in securing "strategic depth" in Afghanistan. The failure of democracy to take firm hold and of robust economic development to take off have contributed crucially to Pakistan's failure to put the struggle with India behind it.

In the midst of the bloodbath of Partition Mohammed Jinnah became the first head of Pakistan's provisional government, set up for the country by the British. It was a constitutional monarchy, to be governed at the start according to the constitution of the Government of India Act of 1935, until a new constitution was passed. Jinnah was appointed governor general, a largely ceremonial position created to serve the interests of the British monarchy, and was also voted president of the Constituent Assembly. Despite constant vilification by Islamists, he continued to forcefully argue for a secular future for Pakistan, and in his most famous speech, in August 1947, he declared, "You may belong to any religion, cast or creed—that has nothing to do with the business of the state."[3] But he died just a year later from lung cancer, leaving the nation in turmoil.

In the absence of Jinnah's strong political leadership, power gradually shifted to the groups pressing for Pakistan to be an Islamic state, and in 1949 the Constituent Assembly adopted a resolution declaring that it was the obligation of the state to enable Muslims to order their lives in accord with the teachings and requirements of Islam, in effect declaring Pakistan to be an Islamic state. This was the first in a series of concessions by the country's secular leadership to the growing power of the Islamic groups.[4]

Even though membership in the Islamic religious parties was not large, they exerted increasing influence. One of the most powerful Islamist leaders was Abu Ala Mawdudi, a leading Islamic scholar of his era, who had founded an Islamist party, Jamaat-e-Islami (JI), in 1941. He was the first to develop a modern political Islamic ideology and a plan for social action to realize that vision. The fundamental objective of JI was to seize state power and establish Islamic rule, though the party pledged not to adopt any illegal or underground means to attain power. "It will educate people in the first course about real Islamic values and [how to] participate in elections," the founding manifesto declared.[5]

Mawdudi was a prolific writer, and in his many books and pamphlets he laid out an elaborate ideological position regarding Islam, arguing that Islam is as much a political ideology as it is a religion and that the basic division in the world was between "Islam and un-Islam." He described the political system of Islam as "theo-democracy," a system in which officials would be elected but would be subject to divine laws interpreted by the theologically learned.

Like other Islamic leaders, Mawdudi had been opposed to Jinnah's demand for the creation of Pakistan, but after the founding he and his party set a new course, joining ranks with other Islamic groups to push for an Islamic constitution. Mawdudi came into heated conflict with the government when he spearheaded a movement to excommunicate a minority Islamic community, the Ahmadiya, from Islam for what most clerics believe to be their heretical refusal to acknowledge Mohammed as the last prophet of God. Mawdudi's followers whipped up public sentiment against the Ahmadiya, calling for their expulsion from government and the military, and widespread riots broke out in Pakistan's largest province, Punjab, in 1953. Hundreds of people were killed in the riots, which were ultimately suppressed by the military.[6]

Mawdudi was arrested and sentenced to death for his role in instigating the riots, but he was freed shortly thereafter due to both domestic and international pressure. He and the JI party continued to gain power, and when the first Pakistani constitution was finally passed in 1956 it accommodated many of the demands of Mawdudi and his allies, declaring the country to be an Islamic republic.[7]

The ethnic, economic, religious, and ideological divisions within the country continued to plague the government after the passage of the constitution. A central problem was the distribution of power between West and East Pakistan. From

1950 to 1958 Pakistan had seven prime ministers. The continuing political instability gave increasing power to the military, and in 1958 Gen. Mohammed Ayub Khan, the commander in chief of the Pakistani armed forces, seized power in a bloodless coup and declared martial law in the country, in the first of what was to be a succession of oscillations between military rule and democracy. He shelved the constitution and ruled by military junta, which brought basic political and economic stability to the country. His regime marked a serious setback for the Islamists.

Ayub Khan pursued a modernizing agenda that opposed the encroachment of religion into politics, and over the course of the following decade the country's political establishment became dominated by the military bureaucratic elite. The JI's offices were closed down and its funds were confiscated, and in an attempt to curtail the powers of Islamic clerics the military regime put mosques and other religious centers under government control. Ayub Khan was attempting to emulate Kamal Ataturk, the founder of modern Turkey, who had introduced wide-ranging reforms there to separate religion from the state and rapidly modernize. However, in Pakistan the divisions within the population and the still largely feudal economic structure, with wealth concentrated in a landowning elite, as well as the determination of the Islamists made reforms more difficult.

As the cold war between the United States and the Soviet Union heated up, Ayub Khan aligned Pakistan with the U.S.-led Western alliance, and the United States began sending massive aid to the country, mostly allocated to the military, which turned Pakistan into a major military power in the region.

Ayub Khan's regime represented a watershed in the development of the country, starting the process of industrialization, improving agricultural production, and forcing through modest land reform.[8] But autocratic rule also generated increasing political unrest, with growing demands for a return to democracy. In recognition of the push for change, in 1962 Ayub Khan forced through a new constitution that officially ended martial law and instituted a hybrid electoral system he called "guided democracy," limiting the franchise to an electoral college.[9] He was elected president in 1964 in elections that were widely believed to be rigged, causing mounting protests. His hold on power was further challenged a year later, when war broke out between India and Pakistan.

Ayub Khan had sent thousands of Pakistani soldiers into Indian-controlled Kashmir, a heated point of dispute between the recently separated countries that remains embroiled in fierce contention and conflict to this day. Kashmir is majority Muslim, and the Partition agreement had provided for a public vote to determine whether the territory would ultimately become part of Pakistan or remain controlled by India. But India never held that vote. Ayub Khan had set his sights on claiming the territory, which Pakistanis widely believed to be a rightful part of their country. India retaliated with a military strike on Pakistan, and a two-week-long war ended with the intervention of the United States and the Soviet Union. A peace agreement was signed between the two countries in Tashkent, arbitrated by the Soviets, which was widely denounced in Pakistan as a humiliating surrender.

Opposition to Ayub Khan's rule built steadily in the following years as his economic reforms failed to substantially improve the living standards of much of the lower classes, and a movement for the establishment of full democracy was spearheaded by a number of opposition parties.[10] Nationwide antigovernment agitations forced Ayub Khan to step down in 1969, handing over power to his chief of army staff, Gen. Mohammed Yahya Khan, who again declared martial law but announced that full, free elections would be held the next year.

Yahya Khan, who had a reputation as an able but debauched officer, stepped back from Ayub Khan's move toward secularization and also scrapped the 1962 constitution, proposing guidelines for a new constitution to be approved by a new Constituent Assembly after the elections, which would stipulate that laws must be in conformity with the principles of Islam and the head of state must be a Muslim. In his public pronouncements Yahya Khan often used such expressions as "the Islamic ideology of Pakistan" and "the glory of Islam," and under his influence the military put its support behind the Islamic political parties, JI primary among them.[11] His strategy was to create an alliance between the military and the Islamists in order to check the rising power of the forces in favor of secular democracy and maintain the preeminence of the military in Pakistani politics.

Even with the backing of the military regime, however, the Islamists failed to mobilize popular electoral support in the 1970 elections, and the regime was shocked that the majority was won instead by a nationalist party in East Pakistan, the Awami League, which championed the secession of East Pakistan into a separate state. The election brought to a head tensions between East and West Pakistan; in the West the Awami League had no support, and the populist Pakistan People's Party of Zulfikar Ali Bhutto emerged as the dominant group. When Yahya Khan refused to hand over power to the Awami League a mass uprising broke out in East Pakistan; thousands of people were killed by the Pakistani Army in what escalated into a civil war.[12]

Millions of Bengalis fleeing the military operation took refuge in the neighboring Indian state of West Bengal, where the Awami League established a provisional government in exile, declaring independence from Pakistan. India had already been involved in the civil war by providing sanctuary to the Bengali freedom fighters, and in mid-December Indian forces entered East Pakistan to aid the secessionists. This military intervention by India led to a humiliating defeat of the Pakistani Army and the establishment of East Pakistan as the separate Republic of Bangladesh.

The country created by Mohammed Ali Jinnah had been torn in two, with profound consequences for the place of Islam in the Pakistani state. With no anchor any longer in South Asia, Pakistan became more closely allied with the Muslim world of the Middle East, and the country's disintegration was used by Islamists as a powerful argument that a secularized Islamic government had failed. A revolt by young army officers in the wake of the war forced Yahya Khan to resign, handing over power to the popular Zulfikar Ali Bhutto.

Bhutto was the scion of a wealthy landowning family from the southern province of Sindh, whose father had been a prominent political figure in the Indian colonial government. Bhutto rose quickly through the ranks of Pakistani politics, serving as foreign minister in Ayub Khan's government, in which capacity he strongly advocated for a tough stance against India. He resigned in response to the humiliating peace treaty, a treaty he had been sent to negotiate but argued against, and following his resignation he founded the Pakistan People's Party (PPP), spearheading a populist movement for democratization. In elections in 1970 the PPP gained a large number of West Pakistan's seats in the Assembly, and Bhutto argued vigorously against conceding to the Awami League's assumption of power. He agreed to become deputy prime minister, sharing power with a Bengali politician, Nurul Amin, as prime minister in a military-sponsored plan that excluded the Awami League. When Bengal broke away and Yahaya Khan was forced to resign, Bhutto assumed the role of president. One year later he became prime minister under a new constitution.

Bhutto was widely seen as a savior of the new Pakistan. His greatest achievement was to push through the passage of a new constitution in 1973, which provided for a parliamentary system of government in which power resided primarily with the prime minister rather than the president, and which established an independent judiciary. Pursuing his populist agenda Bhutto also nationalized all the large industries and financial institutions and strengthened workers' rights, giving more power to the trade unions. He instituted further land reform, limiting the size of holdings and redistributing substantial amounts of land to the peasantry.

In 1972, in the wake of the humiliating defeat in the war with India, Bhutto announced at a secret meeting of scientists a plan to develop an atom bomb, a plan driven both by fear of Indian domination and the desire for prominence in the Islamic world. When India successfully tested its own nuclear bomb in 1974, the Pakistani nuclear program took on more urgency, and Bhutto's role in pursuing nuclear capability became a major source of his immense popularity. But he wasn't popular with all Pakistanis.

The Islamists viewed Bhutto's populism as a direct challenge to the establishment of an Islamic state and rallied against his government. In response Bhutto tried to walk a tightrope between conceding to Islamist pressure and maintaining his hold on power, making many concessions to Islamists that wove Islam more deeply into the fabric of the state.

The new constitution included the declaration that Islam was the state religion and that only Muslims could hold the offices of president and prime minister. The state was also required to provide facilities for the practice and teaching of Islam and was obligated to promote Islamic teachings. To ensure that all laws were in agreement with the principles of Islam a Council of Islamic Ideology was appointed.[13] Bhutto further bowed to the Islamists by officially declaring the Ahmadiya sect to be non-Muslim, which strengthened the hand of the Islamists as the arbiters of the state's views on Islam.[14] The Islamists were not content with these concessions, however, and throughout the Bhutto years, 1971–77, the JI and other Islamic groups worked to destabilize the government. The national elections in March 1977 gave them their best chance to do so.

As his term in office progressed Bhutto fell under increasing criticism. His nationalization of so much of the economy had slowed economic growth, and he had become increasingly autocratic, making use of the coercive apparatus of the state and the intelligence agencies to stifle his opponents. When the father of a prominent dissident leader was killed, Bhutto was accused of ordering the murder, and public protest against his regime swelled. He faced intense opposition in the election not only from the Islamists, but across the political spectrum, and when the election results nonetheless showed a clean sweep for the People's Party the opposition staged violent nationwide protests. JI was at the forefront.

Continuing street violence paved the way for another military coup, and on July 4, 1977, troops surrounded the prime minister's house in Rawalpindi and arrested Bhutto. Martial law was declared once again, this time under the leadership of Gen. Mohammed Zia ul Haq, the army's chief of staff. In a dubious trial Bhutto was convicted by the military regime of the murder he had been accused of ordering, and on April 4, 1979, despite worldwide appeals for clemency, he was executed.

General Zia, who came from a conservative Islamic family, greatly enhanced the prestige of the Islamists and enacted a sweeping Islamization of the military and government. He considered it his duty to propagate the power of Islam in any way he could. He gave the army a new motto: Eman (Faith), Taqwa (Abstinence), and Jihad Fi Sabeelillah (War in the way, or for the sake, of God). Soldiers were ordered to prayers regularly, and prayers were often led by commanders. Zia's Islamization process also extended to the wider Pakistani society and greatly fueled the religious extremism that now grips the country.

Claiming that he had a God-given mission "to purify and cleanse Pakistan," Zia presented himself as a pious and humble soldier of Allah. He believed that Islam was Pakistan's source of salvation, the distinguishing feature that rightfully set it apart from India, and he transformed Jinnah's vision of a liberal Pakistan into a theocratic state.

Within days of assuming power he ordered the examination of all the existing laws to verify their conformity with Islamic Sharia law, and he enforced the Islamic penal code, which included corporal punishment such as severing the limbs of thieves, stoning adulterous women, and whipping consumers of alcohol. The enforcement of the codes was used to dramatically curb civil liberties, especially women's civil rights. The existing law that a defendant was innocent until proven guilty was reversed, putting the burden of proof on the accused, and thousands of people were publicly whipped, tortured in prison, and sentenced to execution by military courts to which there was no appeal. Zia also instituted the Islamization of the education system, with courses in Islam made obligatory for students at all levels.[15]

General Zia had a long association with the JI, and the coup propelled the party to center stage of Pakistani politics. The most powerful positions in his first cabinet were filled by members of the JI, and the party also used its influence to place supporters in the security agencies and other sensitive government departments. Under the instruction of the party leadership many members of its student wing joined the army.

Zia's transformation of the army defied long tradition. Carved out of the British Indian Army, the Pakistani Army had retained British traditions and remained a secular organization. Now Islam was incorporated into the army's organizational fabric, and a strong alliance between conservative officers and the Islamist groups took hold. A substantial change that had been evolving in the social composition of the officer corps contributed to the success of this Islamization. In the past the Pakistani officer corps had been dominated by members of the upper class, but by the 1970s many members of the middle and lower-middle classes from the rural areas of Punjab province, where a devout religious ethos was deeply rooted, had joined. They were very receptive to the Islamic teaching introduced at the Pakistani Military Academy and to the Islamic training and philosophy that were made part of the curriculum at the Command and Staff Colleges.[16] A Directorate of Religious Instruction was established to educate the officer corps on Islam, and questions on Islam became a prominent part of the exams for promotion. Many professional officers who were secular were sidelined, opening up space for those with Islamic leanings to reach the senior command level.[17]

Zia provoked worldwide condemnation for his enforcement of harsh Islamic Sharia laws, including public executions and floggings, as well as for executing Bhutto, and the military regime was diplomatically and economically isolated by the United States and its Western allies. His draconian rule also provoked protest within the country. Thousands of opposition activists were imprisoned and curbs were tightened on media as opposition to the military rule swelled.

General Zia's extremist Islamic worldview played a significant role in his decision to throw Pakistan's support behind the jihadis fighting against the Soviets in Afghanistan. But the Afghan fight also provided him the opportunity to transform from a pariah into a lynchpin in the West's war against communism, as well as to gain enormous prestige in the Muslim world. He actively courted the thousands of militants from all over the Muslim world who flocked to Pakistan, and he referred to the fight against the Soviets as a holy war against the "Godless communists." Militant fighters were recruited largely from the ranks of the traditional religious factions.

Although the ISI fully collaborated with the CIA in organizing the covert war in Afghanistan, Zia was not prepared to give a free hand to the CIA. The ISI not only maintained control on contact with the Mujahideen groups, but also handled the distribution of funds and weapons to them. The training of the Mujahideen was also the sole responsibility of the ISI. The decade-long secret war raised the organization's profile and gave it enormous clout.[18]

The training of the militants brought Pakistani Army officers into direct contact with the radical Islamists. Pakistani military officials were also actively involved in fighting the Soviet forces along with the Mujahideen. "Their mission was to accompany [the fighters] on special operations; they acted as advisers, assisting the commander in carrying out his task," said Brig. Mohammad Yousaf, who headed the ISI operations in Afghanistan from 1981 to 1986. "Their assignment could range from blowing up an oil pipeline or mounting a rocket attack on an airfield to laying an ambush."[19] Many soldiers and intelligence officers were indoctrinated into the cause of jihad.

After Zia's death in a plane crash on August 17, 1988—deemed a probable act of sabotage, the perpetrators of which have never been identified—his successors continued the policy of using militancy as a tool to further Pakistan's regional interests. The ISI began focusing the militants on attacks in Kashmir in 1989, in response to an election there that was widely seen as rigged by Indian authorities. In response to the election, the long-simmering political discontent in the region exploded into a popular uprising against Indian control, and a strong cadre of Pakistani militants joined the fight, supporting the insurgency that continues to roil Kashmir to this day. The West had fully endorsed the Islamic jihad in Afghanistan but became alarmed at the militant activities in Kashmir. The Western consternation did nothing, however, to halt Pakistan's support for the militants.

Though democracy returned to the country that year with the return to power of the PPP and the ascension of Benazir Bhutto as prime minister, a decade of political turmoil followed. Throughout these years, in the late 1980s and 1990s, Bhutto and her party traded power back and forth with Nawaz Sharif, who led a coalition of right-wing and Islamic parties, the Islamic Democratic Alliance, which included the JI and was backed by the military.[20] Neither leader was competent as a manager of the nation, and both became mired in corruption charges. Neither was able to exercise control of either the army or the ISI, which went on to build a state within the state and continued to dominate the country's security and foreign policy.[21]

Benazir Bhutto's power was hobbled from the start. The military, which had executed her father only a few years earlier, found it difficult to hand over to her the reins of government, and to contain her power the military leadership backed the Islamic Democratic Alliance, which constantly agitated against her government. The military made it clear that she was not to deviate from General Zia's policies, particularly on Afghanistan, and the generals continued to oversee Pakistan's foreign policy.

The transition to an elected civilian government was fully supported by the United States, and Bhutto promised to continue Zia's pro-West policy. But tensions between the United States and Pakistan soon developed. Just a few weeks after her coming to power, the last Soviet soldier left Afghanistan and Washington's interest in Afghanistan abruptly waned. For the Pakistani military, however, the war was not deemed finished until the communist government in Kabul was ousted, and the Americans' abrupt withdrawal from support for the militant fighters angered the Pakistani military. Pakistanis blamed the Americans for leaving Afghanistan bleeding, and were intensely resentful that they had to bear the brunt of the responsibility to restore order. Islamabad was left with more than three million Afghan refugees to take care of, with little international help.[22] For the next ten years the West remained aloof from the bloody civil war in Afghanistan and allowed the country to become a sanctuary for al Qaeda.

The tensions between the United States and Pakistan mounted when, in August 1990, the administration of George H. W. Bush clamped sanctions on Pakistan for its nuclear weapons program. The sanctions enraged Pakistan's generals, who felt betrayed by their erstwhile ally, ingraining anti-American sentiments among the officer corps that have continued to influence relations.[23]

Also in August 1990 Benazir Bhutto's first term was cut short. Her youth and lack of experience led to complete failure in providing effective governance, and after just eighteen months in power she was ousted by a military-backed constitutional coup, headed by President Ghulam Ishaq Khan. Her husband, Asif Ali Zardari, who was implicated in widespread corruption, was sent to prison on a litany of graft charges.

The subsequent election that year brought to power Bhutto's main rival, Nawaz Sharif. A scion of a wealthy industrial-ist family from Lahore, Sharif had risen to prominence during Zia's military rule. He assumed power in a much stronger position than his predecessor had enjoyed. But even though he was a product of the military establishment Sharif found himself locked in confrontation with his erstwhile patrons as he tried to assert himself.

In 1992 Sharif appointed Gen. Javed Nasir as director gen-eral of the ISI. The born-again Muslim, who saw himself as an Islamic visionary, widened the ISI's covert operations beyond Kashmir and Afghanistan to India proper. During the period of his command, the ISI was accused of masterminding a series of bomb blasts in the Indian financial capital of Mumbai in March 1993, which killed hundreds of people. The allegation brought a storm of criticism upon Pakistan. The United States threatened to declare the country a terrorist state if cross-border terrorist actions were not stopped, and demanded that Islamabad take immediate action to curb the activities of the Islamic militant groups. The government did curtail the ISI's direct support for the militants, but the help to the Kashmiri groups continued through Islamic parties like Jamaat-e-Islami. The maverick general was sacked after Sharif's government was ousted in May 1993, but support for the militant fighting continued nonetheless.[24]

The elections that followed swept Bhutto back into power, this time with a much larger majority in Parliament. She was much more comfortably placed, with her own party loyalist as president and a more supportive military leadership. But having learned from her previous experience she decided not to antagonize the generals; she followed their script on crit-ical foreign policy issues, including support for the Taliban in Afghanistan. The generals saw support for the Pashtun-dominated Taliban in the battle for control of Afghanistan as a cost-effective means of exerting the long-sought "strategic depth" in the country, but they failed to appreciate what a dangerous game they were playing.

When Bhutto's regime faced another onslaught of corruption charges she was again forced from power, in the elections of 1996. Zardari was again accused of corruption: taking secret kickbacks from airline, power station, and pipeline projects, rice deals, customs inspections, defense contracts, land sell-offs, even government welfare. The country was shocked when, in August 1996, reports emerged about Zardari's purchase of a $4 million 355-acre estate south of London, one of the most expensive stretches of countryside in Britain. The investigation also revealed that millions of dollars received in kickbacks were deposited in Swiss bank accounts. Corruption has been endemic and widespread among Pakistani political leaders, but the alleged scale of Zardari's corruption was shocking. He was said to have accumulated assets worth $1.5 billion through illegal means.[25]

The elections once again brought Nawaz Sharif to power, this time with a large majority, and he proceeded to institute a patriarchal style of government, completely disregarding the democratic mandates. Using Islamic politics to bolster his position, he introduced an Islamic Sharia bill, and his exploitation of religion strengthened the hand of Islamic extremism and led to an upsurge in religious-based violence in the country. Sharif had planned to amend the constitution to declare himself Amirul Mominin (Absolute Ruler of the Muslims), but his ambition was cut short by a military coup.[26]

Tension between India and Pakistan heated up once again in February 1999, when the Pakistani Army's chief of staff, Pervez Musharraf, ordered a covert military operation in the Kargil Mountains of Kashmir without Sharif's approval. Musharraf's main objective was to highlight the Kashmir issue and apply pressure to India to give up the territory. But the incursion brought India and Pakistan to the brink of all-out war, and under pressure from the United States Sharif was forced to make humiliating concessions to India in order to forestall hostilities. An intense confrontation between the Pakistani civilian government and military ensued, which culminated in October 1999 with Sharif firing General Musharraf. Musharraf then staged what he referred to as "a reluctant coup."[27]

Musharraf was no more inclined to alter the strategy of support for the militants in Afghanistan and Kashmir than his predecessors had been. On the contrary, he pursued an even more aggressive policy on Kashmir, stepping up support for the militants who continued to fight the Indian forces there, while also continuing to support the Taliban in Afghanistan. Though he was secular himself, and a liberal officer in the model of Ayub Khan, in the early years of his government the militant groups saw a great increase in recruitment, operating openly under ISI patronage. Training camps proliferated in the northwest territories, and by 2001 Pakistan had become home to twenty-four militant groups that were highly trained and operated with impunity in pursuing both their own internal and external agendas.[28]

Musharraf had been an avid patron of the groups and a believer in the Pakistani strategy of gaining "strategic depth" through them. This powerfully influenced his reluctance to order major operations in the tribal regions even as the insurgency grew ever more powerful and the attacks against the U.S.-led forces in Afghanistan began to turn the tide of the Afghan war and allow the Taliban to rebuild its power. Musharraf also feared that any major military operation in the territories would trigger an internal backlash against his government, particularly in the volatile North West Frontier

Province, where the MMA coalition of Islamic parties had gained control of the government. In addition he faced strong opposition from some senior army officers against any crackdown on militants at the behest of America.

Many officers believed that support for the United States would threaten the military's long predominance over the Pakistani government, and they were also opposed to any crackdown on the militants because they believed the militants had fought courageously for Pakistan. A large number of Pakistani officers also refused to accept that the 9/11 attacks were planned by al Qaeda; they believed it was a "Jewish conspiracy" against Muslims, and many of them considered Osama bin Laden an "Islamic warrior." When Musharraf pledged his allegiance to the U.S. fight, dozens of officers and soldiers quit the armed forces and joined the anti-American resistance in Afghanistan, providing the militants with professional training and logistics.[29] This complex set of reasons let the militant genie out of the bottle.

In 2003 Musharraf continued to collaborate closely with the United States in opposing al Qaeda, but he also continued to resist launching a major military operation in the territories. In February of that year, U.S. authorities handed over a list of fifty-three al Qaeda suspects believed to be hiding in South Waziristan and pressed Musharraf to launch a full-scale military operation, indicating that if decisive action was not taken, U.S. forces would cross the border.[30] Musharraf nonetheless was reluctant to launch a major offensive. The capture of a number of important al Qaeda operatives in the coming months, however, eased those tensions. In March 2003 the alleged mastermind of the 9/11 attacks, Khalid Sheikh Mohammed, also known as KSM, was apprehended in the house of a member of a women's ring of Jamaat-e-Islami in

Rawalpindi, perhaps the greatest coup in the U.S. war on terror. Ranking number three in the al Qaeda leadership, KSM was the chief of the group's military wing.[31]

So significant were the operations that in June 2003 President George W. Bush and President Musharraf jointly announced at Camp David that the al Qaeda network had been dismantled and many of its chief operators had been captured.[32] But both the Bush administration and Musharraf and his top commanders had failed to understand how closely the indigenous Pakistani militant groups had begun collaborating with both al Qaeda and the Taliban in launching attacks, and how the groups were evolving into a more tightly interwoven constellation. Despite all of the successes in the operation against al Qaeda, continuing attacks in the coming years would make clear that al Qaeda could sustain itself by drawing on a steady stream of new recruits, and that the Pashtun-dominated Taliban had a large and growing pool of staunch allies among their Pakistani brethren.

Musharraf and his top commanders had thought they could root out al Qaeda from the territories and drive a wedge between the foreigners and the local tribesmen, but they would soon realize just how misguided that judgment was.

CHAPTER 3

The Perils of Appeasement

The Pakistani government was jolted into recognition of the severity of the rising militant threat by two failed attempts to assassinate Pervez Musharraf in December 2003. On December 14 Musharraf was on his way from an air force base to his official residence in Rawalpindi, the seat of Pakistani military headquarters. While he was talking to his military secretary, seated next to him, a huge blast from explosives planted under the bridge the car had just crossed rocketed his three-ton bulletproof Mercedes into the air. Musharraf miraculously escaped harm when an antijamming device fixed to his vehicle delayed the blast for a few seconds.

Less than two weeks later, on December 25, assailants struck again. Two suicide bombers rammed their explosives-laden vehicles into the presidential cavalcade just a few hundred meters from the site of the earlier attack. These explosions were much more powerful than in the prior attempt, and the armored plating of Musharraf's car was destroyed. Fourteen people were killed and forty-six wounded, and blood and body parts covered the car. An investigation later revealed that

Musharraf was saved only because a third bomber had not arrived on the scene at the assigned time.[1]

The audacious attacks were all the more alarming because they happened right in the heart of the high-security zone, where, supposedly, not the slightest movement could go undetected. In both attempts it was clear that the perpetrators were assisted by experts; they were equipped with tracking and other technology not usually available to local militants. The sophisticated planning involved in the attacks was later traced to al Qaeda in Waziristan.[2]

The investigation concluded that the attacks were masterminded by Abu Faraj al-Libbi, a senior al Qaeda leader, and were executed by members of Jaish-e-Mohammed and a group of Pakistani Air Force personnel.[3] Abu Faraj, a Libyan national, had become al Qaeda's operation chief after the capture of Khalid Sheikh Mohammed and was al Qaeda's key link with Pakistani militants. He was responsible for the planning of many terrorist operations in Pakistan.[4] The incidents offered clear proof that al Qaeda was collaborating with local extremists, and provided more evidence that the militants had developed a significant following among soldiers and lower ranking officials, who played a critical role in the plot.

The revelation of al Qaeda's involvement in the assassination attempts underscored that despite the capture of hundreds of al Qaeda fugitives since 2001, the strength of the network was not flagging. Indeed the attacks almost succeeded in eliminating the most important U.S. ally in the region, raising grave concerns about the security situation in the nuclear-armed Muslim country, and a major question that troubled U.S. policymakers was what would have happened had Musharraf been killed. The prospect of Pakistan's plunging into chaos was a nightmare for the United States; despite inconsistency in his policies in dealing with extremism Musharraf was still seen as a lynchpin in the war against al Qaeda.

For more than two years al Qaeda fugitives had operated freely in South Waziristan and it was beginning to become clear that they had turned the territory into the world's largest al Qaeda command-and-control center and militant training facility. More than fifteen camps, operating under the protection of sympathetic tribesmen, were based there, mostly around the towns of Wana and Shakai.[5] In early 2004 many senior al Qaeda operatives from a number of countries traveled to the remote region to participate in a "terror summit" and, according to reports, at the top of the agenda were plans to carry out attacks on the United States and Great Britain.[6] Al Jazeera aired a videotape showing Osama bin Laden walking through mountainous terrain with Ayman al-Zawahiri, and on the tape the two leaders warned of the real battle yet to come.[7]

Taliban insurgents had also continued stepping up attacks on the U.S.-led coalition forces and their Afghan allies in Afghanistan. U.S. military officials admitted that the number of attacks against their troops not only doubled in 2003, but also became more sophisticated. Having regrouped, the Taliban was now willing to take risks, and Taliban commanders threatened to extend their theater of operations from their strongholds in the southern, southwestern, and eastern provinces to northern Afghanistan. Some Taliban guerrilla attacks had already been reported in the northern provinces of Balkh, Faryab, and Kunduz, where the Uzbek warlord Abdur Rasheed Dostum, his Tajik rival, Atta Mohammad, and the Hazara leader Ustad Mohaqqiq, held sway.[8]

Rather than putting up a last stand in 2001, most Taliban fighters had retreated from the major cities and gone underground, hiding their caches of weapons. With the United

States now preoccupied in Iraq and the Afghans growing increasingly restless over the slow pace of reconstruction, the Taliban and other opposition groups found it relatively easy to find recruits for their anti-American campaign. Missile assaults on coalition bases, hit-and-run attacks on their patrols, and remote-controlled bombs targeting coalition vehicles saw a marked increase.

The Taliban also launched frontal assaults on a number of district headquarters in the southwestern Urozgan and Zabul provinces, occupying the administrative and police centers. American and Afghan government spokesmen even reported a series of attacks by a force of six hundred to eight hundred Taliban fighters in the two provinces, by far the largest concentration of Taliban fighters since the American invasion of Afghanistan.[9] The formation of such a large armed force would not have been possible without local support, and it became obvious that many Afghans were willing to take risks by offering sanctuary to the Taliban fighters. The insurgents were employing the same tactics that had been used successfully by the Mujahideen against the Soviet occupiers.

As the attacks against U.S. forces in Afghanistan grew in intensity, the United States formulated a new "hammer and anvil" strategy to pursue the militants more aggressively from the Afghanistan side, stepping up activities along the border. The United States wanted Pakistan's commitment to deploy troops on the other side of the border to work as the "anvil" part of the operation.[10] Top U.S. commanders made several trips to Pakistan in early 2004 to discuss the new strategy with Musharraf. They were followed in March by George Tenet, the CIA director, who flew to Islamabad carrying intelligence reports about the growing al Qaeda activities in Waziristan. U.S. Secretary of State Colin Powell arrived with an offer to grant Pakistan non-NATO status and the promise of a new aid package. The U.S. military officials in Afghanistan blamed Pakistan for allowing the insurgents sanctuary in the border areas. They suspected that members of the Pakistani Army and the ISI were actively helping the Afghan Taliban with training and weapons. Musharraf was under increasing pressure from the Bush administration not only to stop the Taliban's cross-border attacks on the coalition forces, but also to destroy their sanctuaries. American and Afghan officials claimed that Mullah Omar and other top Taliban commanders were hiding in the western border city of Quetta, which Musharraf vigorously denied.[11] In response to the pressure Musharraf complained that the Americans had not yet delivered on a promise to provide equipment needed to give the Pakistani forces night flying and firing capabilities, and had not made drone Predators, still to be flown by American handlers, available on demand, as had been agreed. "Unfortunately, assistance has not materialized as promised from the United States," said Musharraf later. "Its assets and intelligence took a lot longer to arrive than we were told to expect."[12] There was a widening gap in trust between the allies. U.S. and NATO officials were skeptical of Pakistan's sincerity in curbing the activities of Afghan Taliban insurgents, and Pakistan blamed U.S. policies for the rise of Islamic extremism in the country.

Another reason for Pakistan's initial reluctance to launch military operations in Waziristan was the continued opposition of some top military commanders, including the chief of command for the region, Gen. Ali Muhammed Jan Orakzai, to the use of force in the highly volatile region. General Orakzai was intensely critical of U.S. policy in Afghanistan, and his antipathy toward the United States had intensified during a recent visit to Washington. Even as an official guest he was made to go through a series of screenings and checks at the airport immigration counter on his arrival, and he publicly criticized that behavior as discriminatory.[13]

Still hoping to avoid a major military operation, in February 2004 Musharraf met with a group of tribal elders to try to persuade them to expel the foreigners from their areas. "American forces could enter your areas if the al Qaeda sanctuaries are not dismantled," he told them, reporting that intelligence indicated that five hundred to six hundred al Qaeda fighters were operating from bases in the tribal regions.[14] Though he offered amnesty to the foreigners if they agreed to stop cross-border attacks on the U.S. and Afghan forces, predictably the offer was rejected, and at last Musharraf was left with no choice but to attack. General Orakzai retired from service on March 14, making the launch of operations less controversial for Musharraf. On the next day Musharraf deployed six thousand paramilitary and regular army troops to South Waziristan. The fight they were headed for was fierce.

The toughest fighting took place on March 16 in the towns of Kaloosha and Shin Warsak, just a few miles from the regional capital of Wana, where scores of Arabs, Chechens, and Uzbeks had taken sanctuary. Military authorities suspected that Ayman al-Zawahiri was also hiding there. Dozens of soldiers were killed or wounded, and finding themselves surrounded scores of paramilitary soldiers threw away their weapons and fled for their lives. A large group of soldiers took shelter in a mosque in Kaloosha when they came under fire; among them was a colonel who came out with a Quran on his head, begging for his life. He was let go after the tribesmen stripped off his uniform. "Bullets were flying everywhere. Wrapped in blankets, the tribesmen, armed with rocket launchers and automatic rifles, surrounded the troops," recounted Ehsan Wazir, a local resident, when I visited the village weeks after the incident.

On March 22 the militants struck another deadly blow to government forces when they ambushed an army convoy near the village of Sarwakai, also close to Wana. At the scene of the attack I saw charred, twisted steel strewn along the winding road, and dark smoke still billowed from the wreckage of a smoldering military truck. Not a single soldier in the convoy had survived the lightning strike by the militants, who had taken up positions in the surrounding mountains, home of the Mehsud tribe. The bodies of more than a dozen soldiers were found at the site, and the decapitated bodies of a number of others who had been taken prisoner by the assailants were found near the area days later.

The military had lost more than fifty soldiers in twelve days of fighting concentrated in a fifty-square-kilometer area near Wana. Some militia organized by pro-government tribal elders had joined the government forces, but they had done little to turn the tide. The intensity of the fighting shocked military authorities, who had boasted that the operation would be completed in a matter of weeks. The army had no experience in counterinsurgency operations in such treacherous mountain terrain, and it became clear that they were facing a much stronger and better trained force than they had anticipated, comprising both militants from the local tribes and a large contingent of foreigners.

The leader of the tribal militants was the Waziri commander Nek Mohammed, a tall, charismatic young man with long hair and piercing eyes, who had emerged as one of the most powerful militant commanders in the region. A former madrassa student, he had gone to Afghanistan to fight for the Taliban after an unsuccessful attempt to become a businessman. He fought there against U.S. forces in late 2001 and returned to South Waziristan after the fall of the Taliban regime. Of the al Qaeda–affiliated foreigners, Uzbeks comprised the biggest group, led by Tahir Yuldashev, the head of the Islamic Movement of Uzbekistan, which sought to overthrow Islam Karimov's regime in that country. The Uzbeks were ferocious fighters. They had initially come to take part in the fight against the Soviets in Afghanistan in the 1980s, and following the Soviet withdrawal they remained in the region. The stocky, heavily bearded Yuldashev was assigned by the al Qaeda leadership to train Central Asian militants.[15]

Yuldashev, who was also known in the area as Qari Farooq, was a powerful speaker and regularly delivered sermons in a mosque in Wana, becoming very popular among the tribesmen because of his leadership qualities and fiery speeches. Audio and video recordings of him urging volunteers to come forward for jihad were distributed across South Waziristan. Since the U.S. invasion of Afghanistan he had worked with the al Qaeda and Taliban leadership to carry out raids on U.S. and allied forces there.

In the face of such fierce fighting, the paramilitary soldiers joining in the fight, who were Pashtun locals, deserted the government forces in droves, refusing to fire on their fellow tribesmen. Ratcheting up the intensity, al Qaeda released a videotaped message in which Zawahiri exhorted Pakistani troops to rise in revolt against Musharraf, whom he called a traitor of Islam. The tape reinforced the speculation that the al Qaeda leaders were still hiding in the region. Senior Pakistani security officials said the troops came very close to capturing Zawahiri when they raided an al Qaeda safe house, as the literature and other material seized from the mud compound indicated that al Qaeda's number two man had stayed there. Apparently he had left the place just a few days earlier.

On March 28 the Pakistani forces pulled back from Shin Warsak and Kaloosha after the militants freed twelve soldiers who had been taken hostage during the fighting. Though the government issued a deadline by which the militants had to give up the foreigners, the tribal militants had paid no heed and released the men on their own schedule. The offensive rallied Islamists in the region and more widely against Musharraf's government. The clerics of the powerful Lal Masjid mosque in Islamabad issued a fatwa (a religious edict) that declared the resistance in Waziristan a jihad, and called on the people not to give Islamic burials to the soldiers killed fighting the tribesmen. In obedience to the clerics, many parents of the soldiers refused to receive the bodies of their sons. Public opinion in the region turned more hostile toward the military, and Musharraf had no strategy for winning the public over to his cause. The operation also angered some within the officer corps, and several Pashtun officers were court-martialed for refusing to fight.

The operation was a catastrophic failure, and the new top regional army commander, Lt. Gen. Safdar Hussain, who had taken over from General Orakzai, was blamed for the fiasco, which revealed that he had little understanding of the situation in the tribal region. His commitment to the alliance with the United States was also questionable. A year earlier, when I met him at ISI headquarters, he predicted excitedly that the American forces were going to be bogged down in Afghanistan. "That is what we want," he said then.[16] Little did he know that his own troops would soon be confronted with their own serious challenge.

In the wake of the debacle at Shin Warsak and Kaloosha the military made an abrupt about-face, proposing a truce with the militants. General Hussain flew to Nek Mohammed's home village, near the town of Shakai, on April 24 to sign an accord known as the Shakai Agreement. The signing took place at a grand ceremony at a madrassa in Shakai. Amid roars of "Allah o Akbar" (God is great) from the large gathering of tribesmen, the general hugged and garlanded the man responsible for the killing of Pakistani soldiers just a few weeks earlier. "I congratulate Nek Mohammed and his colleagues on their courageous decision. You are our brothers and your allegiance pledge is exemplary," General Hussain said. The government agreed to pay compensation to the tribesmen for war damages and to free dozens of militants detained during the operation. Nek Mohammed and his militants were granted amnesty and allowed to keep their weapons. The foreign fighters as well were again offered amnesty if they agreed to renounce terrorism and stop cross-border attacks on the U.S.-led forces, but the offer again had no effect.[17]

The Pakistani militants had pledged not to attack government forces, but they were not bound to hand over any foreign fighters, and they too refused any commitment to stop cross-border raids on U.S. and Afghan forces. "We cannot stop our jihad until Afghanistan is free from foreign occupation," declared Nek Mohammed after signing the accord.[18]

Pakistani military authorities justified the peace accord as a reconciliation aimed at "weaning the tribesmen away from al Qaeda," but it was widely perceived as an abject surrender. The United States conveyed to Pakistani officials its serious reservations about the deal, which the Bush administration feared would only allow the militants time to regroup.[19] Nek Mohammed declared the agreement a victory for jihad, emerging a hero. Within a few weeks the militant forces launched a series of attacks on the army, leaving no doubt that the agreement had been a farce.

By early June, as the clashes escalated, it became quite apparent that the military's strategy of seeking reconciliation had completely failed. Musharraf ordered the resumption of the offensive, sending seven thousand more troops to South Waziristan, and the military revoked the amnesty it had granted to Nek Mohammed and the other militant commanders. On June 11 troops backed by air force jets mounted a massive operation in Shakai, and at the same time some six hundred commandos were airlifted in to take control of the hills around Wana, marking the first time the air force was used in an operation in the territories. To apply further pressure on the local tribesmen to give up the foreign fighters, the businesses and shops of Nek Mohammed's Waziri tribe, not only in South Waziristan but also in other areas, were shut down. The renewed offensive also marked the first time that a CIA-directed drone carried out a missile strike in Pakistan.

On June 17, 2004, as Nek Mohammed was talking on a satellite phone to a BBC correspondent in the village of Dhog, three miles outside of Wana, a drone swooped down on him. The attack followed days of surveillance. "Why is this bird following me?" Nek Mohammed was said to have remarked to those he was with when he sighted the low-flying drone as it moved in for the strike.[20] I visited the village a few days later. A Hellfire missile had pierced through a mud wall surrounding the compound where Nek Mohammed had been sitting with a group of supporters. Villagers told me that Nek Mohammed's face bore burn marks and his left hand and leg were blown up. In death he became a legend, the tribesmen calling him a "martyr of faith." His mud grave in Shakai became a shrine, visited by scores of tribesmen every day. "He lived and died like a true Pashtun," read a banner on his grave.

Pakistani military authorities denied any U.S. involvement in the strike, claiming it was carried out by their forces, and U.S. officials were completely silent on the incident. The rules of engagement were very clear at that time: surveillance flights were allowed, but strikes could not be carried out without Islamabad's approval. The strike against Nek Mohammed was well covered by the Pakistani press, and thousands of tribesmen mourned his death.

Nek Mohammed's killing caused a brief respite in the fighting, as the militants temporarily withdrew to remote mountainous areas. But even despite such a large deployment, the army's control of the area was tenuous. The operation had exposed the inadequacies of the Pakistani forces and also caused further strains in Islamabad's relations with Washington. Musharraf publicly blamed the United States for not providing helicopters and other equipment that he said was necessary for the fight. "We were even denied the use of helicopters provided by the United States to Pakistan's Drug Enforcement Agency," he later complained.[21] In a short time the militant forces regrouped under new command.

Abdullah Mehsud, a twenty-nine-year-old former Guantánamo Bay inmate, emerged as Nek Mohammad's successor as the primary militant commander in the region, marking a new alliance between the Waziri and Mehsud tribes, which had long feuded. The offensive was beginning to bring former adversaries together. As a young man Abdullah Mehsud had fought for the Taliban in Afghanistan and lost a leg in a land mine explosion a few days before the Islamic militia seized Kabul in September 1996. He had surrendered, along with several thousand fighters, to an Uzbek warlord who was fighting in alliance with the U.S. and coalition forces in Kunduz in December 2001, and he was later handed over to U.S. military authorities.[22]

At the time of his arrest Abdullah Mehsud was carrying a false Afghan identity card, and while in custody he maintained the fiction that he was a simple Afghan tribesman. U.S. officials failed to uncover the truth that he was in fact a Pakistani with deep ties to militants in both countries. "I managed to keep my Pakistani identity hidden all these years," he boasted in a newspaper interview.[23] He spent some twenty-five months in detention at the U.S. base in Cuba before being released in March 2004. Just a few days after his release he was back in South Waziristan fighting the Pakistani forces, a hero to the militants. "We will fight America and its allies," he said in an interview, "until the very end."[24]

Unlike other tribal commanders, who generally had no formal education, Abdullah Mehsud, whose real name was Noor Alam, had been to college. Many of his close family members, including one of his brothers and an uncle, served in the Pakistan Army, and Mehsud himself had applied for a commission in the army but had been rejected. That was when he joined Afghanistan's Taliban militia. He was a colorful character, with long hair and a daredevil nature, and he was often seen riding on a camel or a horse amid his fighters. "I lead by example, by taking risks and surviving in tough conditions," he told an interviewer.[25]

He often gave speeches in mosques and madrassas to motivate tribesmen to fight the Americans, the government, and the Pakistan Army. "Look, if this man with one leg can fight his enemies, why can't you?" he would exhort his clansmen.[26] He gained national attention in October 2004, when he masterminded the kidnapping of two Chinese engineers working on the construction of a dam in South Waziristan. One of the captives was killed trying to escape, and the other was rescued by Pakistani Army commandos. The army targeted him for capture after the raid, and in November 2004 troops took control of the mountaintop village of Nano, just ten miles from the Afghan border, which served as Abdullah's headquarters, but he fled just before the troops arrived.

His adventurism caught up with him, and his tribesmen and al Qaeda forced him out of his leadership position. A dejected Abdullah Mehsud went to Musa Kila in Afghanistan to join the

Taliban fighting the coalition forces.[27] This was when Baitullah Mehsud rose to prominence. The more level-headed Baitullah was put into the leadership role in place of Abdullah. The two men had fought together against U.S. forces in Afghanistan, but there was also rivalry between them. Baitullah had come out from under Abdullah's shadow as the fighting against the Pakistani forces intensified, and though less flamboyant than the charismatic Abdullah, Baitullah was well respected. He commanded a force of four thousand armed men, including several hundred foreign fighters, mostly Uzbeks and other Central Asians.[28]

Pakistani military officials had established contact with Baitullah and they welcomed his takeover of command. "He was more moderate at that time and had not yet developed a radical agenda," said a senior army officer. Baitullah at that stage appeared amenable to negotiating, and military commanders were convinced that he could be separated from the foreign fighters. But that expectation proved tragically mistaken.

A black-bearded, slow-talking man, called by his followers the emir sahib, or revered leader, Baitullah had risen a long way from his years as a young jihadist during the Afghan civil war. He was born into the Shabikhel clan of the Mehsud tribe in the early 1970s, in a village called Landi Dhok, in the Bannu region of the North West Frontier Province. A large number of Mehsud tribesmen were in the transport business, and Baitullah had worked briefly as a truck driver. He got involved with Afghanistan's Taliban movement at an early age, starting as a low-level commander, and he never went to school or to a madrassa. Semiliterate and only in his late twenties, he fit the mold of a classic Pashtun tribal leader, ruthless and shrewd, but he was also deeply religious.

He had learned the hard lessons of other militant leaders who grew too enamored of the spotlight for their own good, such as Nek Mohammed and Abdullah Mehsud, and he gave no interviews to the media and avoided being photographed. This was an aversion he shared with Mullah Omar, the self-styled spiritual leader of Afghanistan's Taliban movement, to whom he owed his allegiance. His modest ways and humble demeanor gave little indication of the ferociousness he would later become known for.[29]

As the militant forces regrouped under Baitullah's command, the campaign in South Waziristan dragged on. From March 2004 to January 2005 the security forces lost an estimated 230 soldiers, though they did succeed in regaining control of a large part of the region. Better equipment had finally arrived from the United States, including night vision goggles and Bell 4 helicopters, and American instructors had started training Pakistani Army commandos and pilots in night vision flying and airborne assault tactics. But the war was far from over. The troops were confronted with an invisible enemy. "We never know where the next bullet is coming from," a senior officer said.

Army posts had been set up on the mountains surrounding Wana, and troops had gained control of the towns of Laddah, Sararogha, and Makin, as well as the main road through the territory. But the insurgents were still in control of the peripheries, and the traditional administrative system in the tribal area had been undermined. The political agent, through whom the federal government controlled the semi-autonomous region, had been completely sidelined as the army took control. The militants targeted the tribal elders who supported the military operation, killing many of them; most of the rest fled for their lives. Eventually the entire administrative structure was brought down, and the vacuum was filled by hard-line

clerics and militant commanders. Though many of the tribesmen wanted to see the foreigners go, they were now essen-
tially powerless against the militants among them.

Musharraf had failed to mobilize public support for the military operation, and many of his commanders favored another
attempt at reconciliation with the tribes. Following secret
negotiations and a prolonged process of arbitration by the
tribal *jirga*, the military council, a new peace deal was signed
with the militants. The military agreed to withdraw troops
from the checkpoints it had set up in the areas controlled by
Baitullah and to deploy only paramilitary Frontier Corps personnel in the region, who are drawn from the Pashtun tribes
at the five forts there. In return Baitullah agreed not to harbor foreign militants or attack government officials and not to
block development projects. The government also agreed to
pay $540,000 to some of the tribal commanders, money the
militants said they owed to al Qaeda.[30]

The signing ceremony was held on February 7, 2005, at
the historic fort of Sararogha, eighty kilometers from Wana,
and was attended by a thousand tribesmen and senior civil
and military officials. His face covered with a white scarf
to avoid being photographed, Baitullah signed the agreement
amid shouts of "God is great!" and "Death to America!" He
insisted that he was not surrendering to the government. "My
head can be chopped off but it will not bow to anybody. My
head only bows to God five times a day," he told the reporters
covering the ceremony.[31]

The agreement established Baitullah as the undisputed
leader in South Waziristan, allowing him to reassert his control over the areas the militants had lost to the military. The
Pakistan government had effectively handed over control of
the area to the militants. Millions of dollars of U.S. aid for
the development of the tribal areas made its way to Baitul-

lah's supporters, which enabled him to further enhance his power and the size of his fighting force. The money was paid to tribesmen close to Baitullah as a part of the peace deal, as part of the government's plan to wean him away from support for al Qaeda.[32]

Gen. Safdar Hussain declared Baitullah a "soldier of peace" after meeting with him in Peshawar several months after the peace agreement, and claimed that South Waziristan had been cleared of all foreign fighters. But even as the general was claiming victory Baitullah's forces resumed killing tribal elders who had supported the military, and on May 29 militants shot dead a former federal minister and Senator Faridullah Khan, along with two other tribal elders. I had seen Faridullah at an army-sponsored tribal jirga in Shakai a day earlier. Escorted by armed guards, the middle-aged tribal chief, who sported a huge turban and a bushy mustache, had declared that al Qaeda was on the run. "Peace has been restored here by the military," he told me. Now, almost one year after the signing of the agreement, Musharraf declared Baitullah a terrorist and vowed to eliminate him. "We are after him and would kill him if we get an opportunity," he declared at a press conference in late 2006.[33]

The failure of the government's approach was further exposed when it became clear that the insurgency had spread to neighboring North Waziristan, as thousands of foreign fighters fled the offensive in South Waziristan, with al Qaeda leaders turning the territory into their main base. The militants there loyal to Gul Bahadur had also become more active on both sides of the Pakistan-Afghanistan border. On July 14, 2005, U.S. forces fired several missiles on a group of militants loyal to Gul Bahadur who were crossing into Afghanistan, killing twenty-four of them.[34] North Waziristan now became the main target of CIA drone strikes, and on May 14,

2005, a drone attack killed Haithem al Yameni, the first senior al Qaeda member killed by a drone inside Pakistan.[35]

For weeks Haithem had been under aerial surveillance by U.S. intelligence and military personnel working along the Pakistan-Afghanistan border. The U.S. team hoped that he would lead them to Osama bin Laden, but after Pakistani authorities captured the al Qaeda third in command, Abu Faraj al-Libbi, CIA officials became concerned that Haithem, who had been considered a possible successor to Libbi, would go into hiding, so they decided to kill him instead.[36] The drone located Haithem in the village of Toorikhel and fired on him late in the night as he was being driven in a car by a local warlord.[37] Pakistani officials tried to cover up the incident by saying that Haithem and the driver were killed by a car bomb, and his death drew very little attention.

A number of months later, in December 2005, the CIA got its biggest drone catch to date. The target was Abu Hamza Rabia, a thirty-two-year-old Egyptian who was believed to be al Qaeda's senior international operations commander. A close associate of Ayman al-Zawahiri, a fellow Egyptian, Rabia was responsible for training, recruiting, and planning operations outside Pakistan and Afghanistan.[38] He had moved into North Waziristan on instructions from Zawahiri, and he worked as the main al Qaeda coordinator with local tribesmen, acting as the effective head of al Qaeda's operations in Pakistan. Rabia's name had first surfaced during investigations into the two failed assassination attempts on President Musharraf in December 2003; he was thought to be one of the masterminds of the plot. According to Western and Pakistani intelligence sources he was among al Qaeda's top five leaders.

On November 5 a drone fired a missile that struck an al Qaeda safe house near the town of Mirali, in North Waziristan, killing Rabia's wife and daughter and six others, but Rabia escaped with only slight injuries.[39] But the CIA and Pakistani intelligence continued to track him, and just a few weeks after the first attempt another Predator strike killed him. The Pakistani government again vehemently denied that there had been a missile attack, insisting that Rabia was killed by a blast from explosives inside the house. But shrapnel found by local reporters at the scene bore the initials "AGM 114," signifying a U.S. guided missile, confirming that there had been a Hellfire attack.[40]

This was the first time evidence of U.S. missiles came to the surface, which reinforced public suspicion of Pakistan's cooperation in the drone strikes. Suspicions that the government was covering up the drone activity were intensified when, in December 2005, a tribal journalist who had broken the story of the incident, Hayatullah Khan, was pulled from his car by armed men. Six months later his mutilated body was recovered from a desolate area. The Pakistani government denied any involvement of its security agencies, but Hayatullah's family was convinced that the government was responsible for his murder. Two years earlier he had been detained by the U.S. security forces in Afghanistan and interrogated at Bagram Air Force Base on suspicion of being a Taliban ally. He was released after a few weeks but remained under surveillance, and Hayatullah's wife alleged that he was constantly harassed by the intelligence agencies. His family suspected that he was killed after he refused to backtrack on his report that Rabia's death was caused by U.S. Hellfire missiles. A few months after his death his wife too was mysteriously killed, and suspicion again fell on the intelligence agencies.[41] Other theories, though, suggested that Hayatullah may have been killed by Uzbeks or al Qaeda operatives for being a government informant.

The drone operations first generated widespread protest

when the CIA extended the strikes beyond Waziristan. On January 13, 2006, Predators struck Damadola village in the Bajaur tribal region, well north of Waziristan, another of the FATA territories, which had also become a hotbed of extremism. In the early morning hours several Predators circled the village before launching four Hellfire missiles into a mud-walled compound. The attack razed three houses and killed twenty-two people, mostly women and children, the deadliest strike yet.[42]At least fourteen of the victims were from just one family. Shah Zaman, a local resident, recalled to me how he ran with his wife toward a nearby mountain for shelter when the first missile struck the compound next to his house. Three more explosions followed, one blasting his house and killing his two sons and a daughter and reducing his house to a heap of mud. Everything within a hundred-yard radius was blackened.[43]

Nestled among high peaks, Damadola, which lies just five miles from Afghanistan, was suspected to be a hideout of Ayman al-Zawahiri. It was an ideal base for militants. The Pakistani Army had never set foot there, and it was the stronghold of a pro-Taliban militant group led by the charismatic Faqir Mohammed. Shin Kot, a small village just south of Damadola, had hosted al Qaeda's headquarters in the winter of 2005–6, and the area featured an elaborate network of mountain caves that served as al Qaeda's nerve center.

The strike on Damadola was apparently launched after the CIA received ground intelligence that Zawahiri and other senior al Qaeda operatives were invited to a feast there for the holiday of Eid al Adha. The fifty-four-year-old Egyptian doctor had been on the run for more than four years despite a $25 million bounty on his head,[44] and Pakistani security officials believed that he constantly moved through the forty-square-kilometer area along the border. He was known to have regularly visited the Damadola area, and some believed he had even married a local girl. Reports suggested that CIA officials may have waited too long for confirmation of his presence and decided to strike when the al Qaeda leader had already left the place. Unlike in the past, Pakistani authorities were not consulted and were informed of the pending attack less than one hour before it occurred.[45] According to security officials at least four al Qaeda operatives were among the dead, though they were never identified as their supporters took away the bodies within hours of the attack.[46] Villagers later confirmed that their Eid guests had included four men who had come from Afghanistan, but they insisted that none of them was a high-level al Qaeda official.[47]

The dead were buried the next day amid angry protests. Tribesmen blocked roads and burned down the office of Associated Development Construction, a U.S.-funded nongovernmental organization in Bajaur, a sign of increasing frustration over the raids and the killing of civilians. The strike sent a shockwave across the country, greatly fueling anti-American sentiment.

On January 15, 2006, thousands of people in Karachi joined a protest against the Damadola attack in one of the largest anti-American rallies since Pakistan joined the war on terror in 2001. A highly charged crowd chanted "Death to America!" and "Stop bombing innocent people!" Organized by right-wing Islamic groups, the rally badly shook the government.

Once again the Pakistani government tried to cover up the CIA's role in the attack, insisting that it was carried out by its own security services, but mounting public outrage forced the government to backtrack. The Foreign Ministry condemned the raid and lodged a formal protest to the U.S. ambassador, Ryan Crocker, over the loss of innocent lives. But at the same time Musharraf also warned people not to harbor militants.

"If we keep sheltering foreign terrorists here . . . our future will not be good," he said in a speech broadcast on state television.[48]

There was no public comment from U.S. officials on the incident. Some political figures, such as Senator John McCain, said they regretted the death of civilians, but they also defended the strikes. "We apologize, but I can't tell you that we wouldn't do the same thing again. We have to do what we think is necessary to take out al Qaeda, particularly the top operatives," McCain declared, reflecting the Bush administration's firm view on the CIA operations.[49]

In a video message released a couple of weeks later, on January 30, 2006, Zawahiri came out with a stinging tirade against the U.S. and Pakistani governments for killing innocent people. Sporting his trademark white robes and white turban, the al Qaeda second in command vowed to avenge the deaths. More widespread protests were triggered when the Pakistani security forces raided a suspected hideout in the village of Danday Saidgai, killing forty-one suspected militants. U.S. Special Forces were reportedly involved in the assault, fueling heated protests in the city of Miranshah, the regional headquarters.[50]

Heavily armed tribesmen then attacked a paramilitary fort and army installation in Miranshah, seizing government offices and the local telephone exchange and cutting off communication with other parts of the country. Armed insurgents patrolled the streets of the town as the paramilitary troops were withdrawn, and the army headquarters in Miranshah came under heavy attack. On March 4 the troops retaliated, using heavy artillery and helicopter gunships, killing more than a hundred militants in the bloodiest battle to date in North Waziristan.

On the same day President Bush arrived in Islamabad amid

massive security. The city was heavily fortified with some ten thousand troops and a huge police deployment. A day earlier, on March 5, a suicide bomber had rammed his explosives-packed vehicle into a car outside the U.S. Consulate, killing an American diplomat. While praising Musharraf for his "courage" Bush also urged his ally to do more to stop the infiltration of Taliban insurgents into Afghanistan. Musharraf was visibly uncomfortable as he stood beside Bush at a joint press conference and heard the U.S. president questioning his commitment to fighting the war on terror. "Part of my mission today was to determine whether or not the president is as committed as he has been in the past to bringing these terrorists to justice," [51] Bush said. The president's pointed comments reflected Americans' growing frustration over Musharraf's failure to stop Taliban insurgents from using Pakistan's territory as a base for the attacks on the coalition forces in Afghanistan. More American soldiers were killed in early 2006 than in the previous four years following the U.S. invasion in December 2001.[52] It was quite an embarrassing moment for Musharraf, who had put his life at stake by supporting the United States.

A day earlier, in New Delhi, the U.S. president had hailed India as an emerging power and awarded it an unprecedented civilian nuclear technology deal. Now all Musharraf got was a lecture on getting tougher with the Taliban and vague promises of future military technological assistance. Although Pakistan remained central to U.S. security interests in the region, this raw deal raised further skepticism in the Pakistani military about America's long-term commitment to their country.

Despite the pressure from the United States to ramp up operations against the militants, in a surprising move in May 2006 Musharraf appointed retired General Orakzai as governor of the North West Frontier Province and also the administrative head of the tribal region. Orakzai had long been

opposed to military action against the militants, and he immediately began negotiating with them. On September 5 he
signed a truce with the militants in North Waziristan, led by
Gul Bahadur and another tribal leader, Abdul Khaliq, who had
led the fight against the military. The Waziristan Accord, as it
was known, put an end to all army operations in the territory,
and troops were pulled back from the security checkpoints to
their barracks. The government also not only released all militants captured by the military, but agreed to pay compensation to those killed during the fighting, effectively legitimizing
their activities.

To help sell the deal to Washington, Musharraf took General Orakzai to the Oval Office several weeks later. In his
presentation to President Bush, Orakzai advocated a strategy that would rely even more heavily on cease-fires and said
that striking deals with the Taliban inside Afghanistan would
allow U.S. forces to withdraw from Afghanistan within seven
years. Bush supported the deal, claiming that it would not create safe havens for the Taliban and could even offer "alterna-
tives to violence and terror," but he added, "You know we
are watching this very carefully, obviously." Three months
later the U.S. State Department publicly declared the deal a
failure.[53]

Musharraf had approved the controversial deal despite the
warning from some of his senior generals that it would carry
serious consequences for the country's internal security. "The
deal left pro-government tribal leaders at the mercy of the
militants," said a senior general who blamed Musharraf for
the disastrous results. "The spread of militancy which swept a
large part of the northwestern province was largely the result
of this policy of appeasement."[54] Lt. Gen. Hamid Khan, the
regional corps commander, was among the officers who had
strong reservations about General Orakzai's approach, a view

that cut short his tenure as commander. In less than one year he was sent back to General Headquarters.

One of the reasons for Musharraf's decision to pull back the troops from Waziristan was a growing rebellion in the western province of Balochistan. The federal government had long ignored the demands of nationalists in the province for greater political and economic autonomy, and tensions had started mounting a few years earlier, when the military government announced its intention to set up three new installations in the province. The move was seen as a means to tighten federal control. The long-simmering political unrest exploded into insurgency in August 2006, after the military killed nationalist leader Akbar Khan Bugti, who had also served as the governor of the province. The protest against his killing turned into violent attacks on security forces and defense installations. Some analysts suggested that Musharraf approved the Waziristan deal in order to take care of "an even bigger security problem."[55]

Whatever his reasons for making the deal, this was yet another peace accord that was to prove ill-fated. The tribal militants had pledged not to allow foreign fighters in their midst or to run cross-border operations, but they violated those pledges from the outset. Officials from the United States watched with alarm as the number of cross-border attacks actually increased substantially. In the months after the agreement was signed cross-border incursions from the tribal areas into Afghanistan rose by 300 percent.[56] In the spring of 2006 the Taliban launched an offensive in southern Afghanistan, increasing suicide bombings sixfold and U.S. and NATO casualty rates by 45 percent.[57] At the same time they assassinated many more Pakistani tribal elders who were cooperating with the government.

In November 2006 Lt. Gen. Karl Eikenberry, head of U.S.

forces in Afghanistan, warned that the number of Taliban attacks out of North Waziristan had tripled since the deal was signed, and on December 26 U.S. Assistant Secretary of State Richard Boucher said, "The Taliban have been able to use the tribal regions for sanctuary, and for command and control, and for regrouping and supply." [58] Nonetheless the Pakistani government continued to stick to the terms of the deal until well into 2007, exacerbating tensions between the two governments. Relations were further strained when the CIA carried out another drone strike in November 2006, on a village just three kilometers from Damadola.

Just before dawn the residents of Chinagai, a small border village in the Bajaur tribal area, woke to a thunderous blast. Before they realized what had happened three more explosions ripped through the village. The lightning missile attack reduced a local madrassa, Zia-ul-Uloom, into a massive pile of rubble. Some eighty-five people died in the deadliest ever single drone attack. [59] The site was strewn with mutilated bodies, the shoes and clothes of young children scattered all over. Many bodies were burned beyond recognition. A large number of the victims were said to be members of a pro-Taliban organization called Tehreek Nifaz Shariat Mohammadi, and they were reportedly there to attend a tribal assembly due to take place the next day to approve a peace deal with the government. [60] But exactly who was killed in Chinagai remained unclear. Local residents and some survivors claimed that several children, some as young as seven, were among the dead.

The Pakistani government once again tried to cover up the CIA's involvement by claiming responsibility for the bombing. Defending the raid, Pakistani military officials claimed that the madrassa was being used as a facility to train suicide bombers. Musharraf contended that those killed in the madrassa were not innocent: "They were militants doing military training. We were watching them for the last six or seven days . . . who they are and what they are doing."[61] The military described the attack as "a major counter terrorist operation," and security officials announced that it was conducted on the basis of solid intelligence information provided by the Americans, as well as local informers.[62] Apparently U.S. drones had been flying over the area for several days before the attack and had picked up some extraordinary activity inside the compound. Roughly a hundred men were undergoing some kind of guerrilla training on the campus, which was usually closed down during the Ramadan and Eid holidays.

A high-resolution camera also detected a middle-aged bearded man delivering a lecture to the trainees. U.S. and Pakistani intelligence officials thought he could be Ayman al-Zawahiri or Abu al-Obaida al-Misri, as both al Qaeda leaders regularly frequented the mountainous region. Misri was believed to be the mastermind behind the plot to blow up passenger aircraft flying out of Heathrow International Airport.[63]

The strikes had been carried out with the consent of the Pakistani government, and they made clear that Musharraf had run out of options to control his lawless western border.[64] He appeared to have no coherent plan, switching back and forth from negotiating with the tribesmen to attacking them.

The backlash against the raid was even stronger and more widespread than that after the Damadola strike. Thousands of heavily armed protesters took to the streets in the biggest antigovernment demonstrations ever seen in the volatile border areas. The attack proved to be a potent propaganda tool for the militants. Islamists seized on the attack to whip up antigovernment and anti-American sentiment. The militants' retaliation was swift and brutal. Several days later, on November 8, 2006, a chador-clad young man blew himself up in the middle of the parade ground at the Punjab Regiment Center in Dargai, a town in the restless North West Frontier Province. Some two hundred recruits had assembled there for morning training; an estimated forty-two of them were killed and dozens of others wounded in the first such attack on a military garrison.[65]

A major concern for Musharraf was how to defuse the mounting public anger about the strikes. The madrassa attack had not only provoked strong antigovernment reaction among Pakistan's border-dwelling Pashtun tribal groups, but anger had also spilled over to parts of the North West Frontier Province, where Musharraf's pro-U.S. policies were already unpopular. There was growing fear that the anger would sweep other parts of the country as well.

Musharraf had wedged himself between a rock and a hard place by taking the blame for the strike. The most serious threat he faced was that any further military operation in the border areas could split the army, which was clearly unhappy at the prospect of fighting their own people. Hundreds of soldiers had already been killed in the military campaign in Waziristan, and discontent within the army ranks was growing. At least six middle-ranking army officers were court-martialed for refusing to fight.

The on-again-off-again policy of appeasement had been an abysmal failure, drawing increasing criticism from U.S. and coalition commanders in Afghanistan as well as the Afghan government. The Bush administration had been willing to give Musharraf's new peace approach a chance, but other U.S. officials were much more critical of the truce. "Taliban and al-Qaeda leaders in Waziristan have developed a complex cooperative relationship," Lt. Gen. Karl W. Eikenberry, the outgoing U.S. commander in Afghanistan told the House Armed Services Committee in February 2007. "A steady, direct attack against the command and control in Pakistan in sanctuary areas is essential." [66] In her congressional testimony Secretary of State Condoleezza Rice said, "President Musharraf . . . has to do something." [67]

General Orakzai struck back at the criticism by accusing Western allies of scapegoating Pakistan for their own failures in Afghanistan. Talking to a group of journalists in February 2007 he declared the Taliban insurgency to be a "war of liberation" fought by disaffected tribesmen and that enjoyed broad public support. "For all the sacrifices we have rendered in the war on terrorism there is hardly any acknowledgement," he said. [68]

Musharraf was confronted with tough choices: to send a reluctant army back to fighting in the tribal areas, risking accusations that innocent civilians were killed, or to strike more peace deals, giving the militants further opportunity to intensify cross-border attacks inside Afghanistan. It was a classic catch-22 situation: he was caught between the rising militancy, a disenchanted army, and the demands of the United States, a very tight spot indeed.

Musharraf continued to ignore the increased activity of the self-styled Islamic vigilante groups operating in the North West Frontier Province and adjoining tribal regions. The administration and the military failed to appreciate the degree to which rising extremism among the Pakistani militant groups had taken on a life of its own. They willfully looked the other way rather than confront clear signs that the extremism of the Taliban was taking root in the territories.

CHAPTER 4

The Holy Terror

On April 28, 2007, Interior minister Aftab Ahmed Khan Sherpao, a burly man in his late fifties, had just finished a speech at a crowded compound in his home town of Charsada, in the North West Frontier Province, when a young man rushed toward him. As a guard blocked the man's way a huge explosion shook the compound and mayhem ensued. Sherpao escaped with only minor injuries, but twenty-eight people were killed.

The assassination attempt on the interior minister, who controlled the internal security of the state—in his own home district no less—spoke volumes about the worsening security situation in the country and the Taliban's growing power in the North West Frontier Province. This was the third high profile suicide attack targeting senior government officials in the past two months. On February 3, three government officials were killed when their car was blown up outside the town of Mir Ali in North Waziristan. Then, on February 6, a suicide bomber blew himself up at Islamabad airport after he was challenged by the security guards close to the VIP lounge. There were fewer casualties in that attack than in the attempt against Sherpao, but it signalled the arrival of the insurgency in the leafy capital city nestled up against the foothills of the Margalla mountains.

In early 2007 a Pakistani Interior Ministry report declared that the Taliban and other Islamist militant groups had not only grown in strength but had spread beyond their strongholds in the tribal regions. "Without swift and decisive action they could destabilize the entire country," Sherpao, told the National Security Council meeting presided over by President Musharraf in June 2007.[1] Sherpao's narrow escape in the suicide bombing in April may have caused him to come out against the government's policy of appeasing the militant groups. His comments pointed to a phenomenon that had gone largely unremarked over the preceding two years: the rise of a distinctive Pakistani Taliban. "The ongoing spell of active Taliban resistance has brought about serious repercussions for Pakistan," he said. "There is a general policy of appeasement towards the Taliban, which has further emboldened them." He asked the government to review its soft policy on militancy and warned about an emerging nexus among the clerics of the powerful Lal Masjid in Islamabad, Baitullah Mehsud in South Waziristan, and a militant cleric, Mullah Fazlullah, who was leading an Islamic insurgency in the Swat Valley of the North West Frontier Province. This was the first public acknowledgment from the Pakistani government of the danger of the militant threat.

Emboldened by the government's ambivalent efforts to suppress the militant threat, Islamic radicals stepped up their activities. Following the peace accord in September 2005 a number of Islamist militant groups had joined Baitullah Mehsud in his mission to create an indigenous Taliban movement and had established an autonomous Islamic Emirate of

Waziristan, inspired by the ousted Taliban regime in Afghanistan. Most of them were breakaway factions of outlawed militant groups like Jaish-e-Mohammed, Lashkar-e-Jhangvi, and Harkat-ul-Mujahideen.

Meanwhile Taliban militias had emerged in several other tribal regions, such as Bajaur, Mohmand, Orakzai, and Khyber. In North Waziristan the group was headed by Gul Bahadur and Maulana Sadiq Noor, and in Bajaur it was organized under Malwi Faqir Mohammed, a firebrand cleric. Similar groups were formed in parts of the North West Frontier Province, including the Swat Valley and Dir districts. The groups operated autonomously, with no central command, and they did not report to the Afghani Taliban.[2] The provincial administration, controlled by the Muttehida Majlis Amal (MMA), gave them its tacit support, and as their power grew they unleashed a reign of terror in many parts of the territories.

It was a scene from hell. A line of bullet-ridden bodies strung from electric poles; a severed head with currency notes shoved into the mouth, rolling on the ground; a dead dog thrown on top of a pile of mutilated bodies in a crowded bazaar. "This is the fate of criminals and of those who disobey God," thundered a long-bearded mullah as he hit one of the corpses with the butt of his rifle.[3]

The gruesome killing had been carried out in December 2005 on the streets of Miranshah, the largest town in North Waziristan. Local Taliban militants had killed some two dozen alleged criminals, leaving them hanging for days in the city center, in the full view of the military and government officials, subsequently tying the corpses to vehicles and dragging them through the streets in a show of medieval barbarism. Tribesmen had gathered in the city center to applaud the killings with shouts of "Allah ho Akbar" (God is the greatest). Videos of the killings were widely circulated in the area as part of the campaign of terror.

The scene was reminiscent of Kandahar, Afghanistan, in 1994, when a group of men led by Mullah Omar lynched a warlord and his henchmen for killing a boy after raping him. That incident had heralded the formation of a Taliban militia, which two years later captured the Afghan capital, Kabul, and established its repressive regime.

A group of radical clerics in Miranshah, operating under the leadership of Gul Bahadur, recruited a militia, composed mostly of students from the local madrassas, which moved to enforce rigid Islamic Sharia rule on the town and the surrounding area. They imposed taxes in line with Sharia practices and banned television, declaring it un-Islamic. "Opium and alcohol have destroyed the youth. Obscenity, video and satellite dishes are everywhere. The government is not taking the responsibility to eradicate these evils, therefore, we decided to put an end to it," declared Gul Bahadur.[4] Any defiance led to harsh punishment. "There was a complete reign of terror," said Rehmat Khan, a resident of Miranshah, who, like scores of other residents, had taken refuge in the town of Bannu, thirty miles away. "No one can dare to challenge them."[5]

The Pakistani military and civil authorities looked the other way during the public hangings. "Their actions had popular support," said Syed Zaheer-ul-Islam, the political agent in North Waziristan, when questioned on the government's inaction on the local Taliban's rule of terror.[6] The local administration was under instructions from the military not to impede the local Taliban, and the government's abdication steadily conceded more and more administrative control to the militants.

The military was awakened to just how serious a threat the Pakistani Taliban had become when, in March 2006, armed with heavy machine-guns and rocket launchers, Taliban militants seized key government buildings in Miranshah, including the telephone exchange, and attacked military posts, killing several government soldiers. The base from where the militants launched their attacks was a local madrassa, known as Gulshan-e-Ilm. Finally Pakistani officials, who in the past had drawn a line between local Islamic militants and foreigners, realized that there was an emerging nexus between the two.

Steadily self-styled vigilante groups started emerging in other tribal regions, and Sharia law was declared by Baitullah Mehsud and Malwi Nazir, another Waziri commander in South Waziristan. In Wana the local Taliban set up offices for recruitment as well as for administering justice, and they issued orders regularly on loudspeakers at local mosques. Video shops were shut down, as well as Internet cafés, both declared un-Islamic, and barbers were ordered not to shave beards. People were prohibited from playing music, even at weddings, and the traditional holiday fairs were banned. Warnings regularly announced that defiance of any kind would not be tolerated. After the local radio station ignored repeated warnings to stop playing music programs it was blown up. Pro-government members of tribal councils, through whom the federal government exercised authority, were either killed or driven out by the militants.

In Dera Ismail Khan, a town in the North West Frontier Province, the local zealots forcibly stopped people from organizing their spring festival and told them to hold a religious conference instead. "We will use other methods if you don't heed our warning," declared a local Taliban leader.[7] Girls schools became a main target of attacks as female education was considered un-Islamic. Scores of schools across the

NWFP and the FATA tribal region were burned down, and similar vigilante actions were witnessed in five other tribal regions: Khyber, Orakzai, Bajaur, Kurram, and Mohmand.

The emerging vigilante groups mostly came from the ranks of the mainstream Islamic political parties that had gained power in the region and were supported by the political leadership of the six-party MMA alliance. In July 2005 the MMA-dominated NWFP Provincial Assembly had passed a controversial Hisba (accountability) law, which stipulated that a watchdog body be set up to ensure that people respected calls to prayer and did not engage in commerce at the time of Friday prayers and that unrelated men and women did not appear together in public places. The law also prohibited singing and dancing. The enactment of the law was stopped by a ruling of the Supreme Court of Pakistan, which declared it unconstitutional, but the MMA government continued to back the militants in their mission.

The Pakistani Taliban was even more brutal than their Afghan comrades. Beheadings and public executions of opponents and government officials became common practice, and videos of those killings were distributed widely to spread fear. Such sadistic acts were unheard of in Pashtun culture, and the brutality was thought to be influenced by Arab and Uzbek militants.[8]

Moving out of the tribal territories, the Taliban quickly established parallel authority in large parts of the North West Frontier Province as well. They were active not only in the remote rural areas, but also in the cities. Self-styled vice squads, mostly comprising students of local madrassas, emerged in various towns enforcing the ban on music, and video and television shops were routinely attacked. The provincial capital of Peshawar was besieged by the Taliban, and the political management of the province, already difficult, became impossible as large pockets of the territory fell under Taliban dominance. One such area was the Swat Valley.

Once a relatively liberal region, dotted with ski resorts and fruit orchards and known for its dancing girls, who performed at most wedding parties and other ceremonies, the Swat Valley is just one hundred fifty miles from Islamabad. Militant violence swept the lush green alpine territory in 2006, when a long-haired firebrand young cleric there, Mullah Fazlullah organized his own Islamic militia. A school dropout, Fazlullah had worked as a chairlift operator at Pakistan's only ski resort, in the town of Malam Jabba in the Swat, before joining the movement for enforcement of Sharia rule. Ironically, in 2008 his supporters would destroy the resort in their campaign against any kind of entertainment they considered un-Islamic.

Fazlullah established a large madrassa in his home village of Imamdehri, which he also used as his headquarters. After leading Friday prayers there he would emerge on a white horse so that the townspeople could have a glimpse of him. "I am following the legacy of Prophet Mohammed," he would say about his habit of horse riding.[9] Popularly known as Mullah Radio, for his fondness for broadcasting his sermons, he and his associates had set up at least thirty-two FM stations in the region, broadcasting his jihadi messages around the clock. He was a formidable leader and developed a large following.

In 2002 he took over the leadership of the outlawed organization Tehfuz Nifaz-e-Sharia Mohamadi after the arrest of its founder, Maulana Sufi Mohammed, his father-in-law. The white-bearded, diminutive Sufi Mohammed, then in his mid-seventies, was arrested and sentenced to five years in prison in 2002 after he took ten thousand men with him to Afghanistan to fight against the U.S. forces. A former local leader of Jamaat-e-Islami, Sufi Mohammed had led an armed insurgency in the Swat years earlier, in 1995, demanding the enforcement of Sharia laws. The revolt was brutally crushed by the security forces, and Sufi Mohammed disappeared from public, resurfacing only after the 2001 U.S. invasion of Afghanistan. Fazlullah had joined Sufi Mohammed and his fighters in Afghanistan. As he now took charge of the new Talibanization campaign, he received the support of many provincial ministers.

Ironically, most of the listeners to his sermons broadcast on FM radio were women. Because work was so hard to come by in the Swat Valley, a large number of men worked far away in the Middle East or in other parts of Pakistan, and Fazlullah understood that winning the support of the women in the area would be an effective strategy. He exhorted them to pull their daughters out of the government-run schools, which he described as the "center of all evils," and so thousands of girls were yanked from school. "Women are meant to fulfill their responsibilities inside their houses. Only in case of dire need they can come out in a veil," he would say in his radio addresses.[10] Women donated their jewelry and savings to him and persuaded their husbands to grow a beard and say their prayers regularly. They even supported Fazlullah's mandate that children should not be inoculated with the polio vaccine, which he claimed was un-Islamic. "To cure a disease before its onset is not in accordance with Sharia laws," he declared. "You would not find a single child to drink a drop of [the vaccine] anywhere in Swat."[11]

In a short time Mullah Fazlullah's followers set up parallel administrations in fifty-nine villages around the Swat Valley, establishing Islamic courts that imposed Sharia law. They also began killing those who publicly opposed them. Among those slain was a local dancer known as Shabana. Her body was dumped in the square in the center of the town of Mingora; the radio proclaimed, "She deserved death for her immoral character." Amjad Islam, a schoolteacher in Mingora, was shot dead for refusing to pull up his *shalwar* above his ankle, which the militants believed was against the Sharia. On January 13, 2007, some eighty gunmen kidnapped Malak Bakht Baidar, a local businessman, from his home in the village of Imagarahi. A member of a politically influential family, Baidar was well-known for his anti-extremist views, and he actively opposed Fazlullah. Days later his mutilated body was found dumped outside the village. This was the first in the series of killings of progressive political activists by the Taliban in the valley.

In the next two years they went on to kill more than three hundred political workers, mostly belonging to the Awami National Party, a progressive Pashtun nationalist party that traditionally had strong political support in the valley. The systematic elimination of political opponents left only the options of surrendering to the Taliban's authority or fleeing to safety. Residents of Mingora, the main town in the Swat Valley, would often wake to find the bodies of those executed by the militants hanging from electric poles in the town's central square, in the full view of the military, with a note of warning not to remove them until midday. Many of those executed were women; their bodies were thrown into the square, which became known as Zibahkhana Chowk, or Slaughter Square. Bakht Zeba, a former member of the Swat district council, virtually signed her death warrant when she criticized the Taliban for preventing girls from attending school. In December 2008 masked gunmen dragged her out of her house, brutally thrashing her before shooting her in the head. Her body lay there for several hours. Educated women like Zeba were specifically targeted. The names of those who had already been executed by the Taliban for violating their decrees and those they planned to kill next were broadcast every night, and terrified residents would listen to the transmission to find out if any of their kin were on the dreaded list.

A large number of police officers and local officials left their jobs, fearing for their lives as the writ of the state collapsed. Scores of police officers were killed by the militants, most of them beheaded. Their decapitated bodies were exhibited to inculcate fear among others. In some cases police and local government officials placed advertisements in local newspapers, announcing that they had resigned from their jobs. "It is the only way a man can save his family's and his own life," remarked a police officer who deserted his post. The absence of any government left an open field to the militants.

The strength of support for Fazlullah was not due only to religious conviction. The government had done little for many years to address economic problems that plagued the valley and the tribal territories. The Swat was one of the poorest regions in the country, with little opportunity for economic advancement. Most of the agricultural land and fruit orchards were owned by a few big landlords, and the government had never made any genuine attempt to change the oppressive system. Fazlullah's followers were not only students of local religious seminaries; a number of jobless school dropouts with little hope of a better economic future joined the cause, as well as impoverished peasant farmers. A major target of Swat militants was the rich landlords. As the campaign of terror commenced most of them fled their homes, and their orchards and lands were distributed among the peasants. This promise of social and economic revolution was a powerful draw.

Khan Gul, a poor farmer from Swat's Matta district, a Kalashnikov resting in his lap and two hand grenades sticking out from the side pockets of his long shirt, told me he had joined Fazlullah's militia in the hope that he would obtain his own piece of land. "He will give us justice," Gul said. Indeed the turmoil in the Swat Valley raised the chilling prospect for Pakistan that the Taliban's takeover there would evolve into a national social revolution, with mullahs leading peasants in the seizure of property from rich landlords all around the country.

The rise of Pakistani Taliban groups presented the greatest threat yet to the power of the traditional tribal system in the territories. Taliban councils started replacing the old tribal jirgas (assemblies), which often led to clashes between the tribesmen and the militants. The Taliban were better organized and armed and they easily managed to marginalize the pro-jirga tribesmen. In many cases jirgas were bombed, killing hundreds of people, and the fear of suicide attacks scared tribal elders away from holding any kind of social gathering. The Taliban also blew up many shrines of Sufi saints, highly revered by Pashtuns.

The rapidly spreading Taliban insurgency terrified many in Pakistan, who saw it as a shocking encroachment, and they were appalled that the government had allowed the Taliban to gain power in an area so close to the country's heartland. Anger at the Musharraf government's mishandling of the rise of militancy swelled. Certainly in the U.S. war on terror few leaders had produced results like Musharraf. His security agencies had captured and delivered to the United States several of the most wanted al Qaeda terrorists. However, his failure to show the same kind of resolve when it came to dealing with the Islamic militancy at home now caused a mounting chorus of criticism of his regime, both within the country and around the world, and despite the backing of the army and the United States Musharraf was faltering. He had spawned a system that was a hybrid of military and civilian rule; now it was beginning to crumble under the weight of its own contradictions. And he was becoming increasingly autocratic.

In particular Musharraf faced intense criticism for the growing high-handedness of his security agencies. Hundreds of people had been picked up as reputed radicals but were never formally charged or brought before the courts, and their detentions were never acknowledged by the military or the government. Many of the detainees were from the western province of Baluchistan, where the government still faced a simmering insurgency. Most of them were opposition political activists, students, and intellectuals. In the face of increasing protests of these draconian measures, and as Musharraf's hold on power weakened, the Supreme Court and its chief justice, Iftikhar Mohammed Chaudhry, started asserting power, taking a stronger position on human rights cases.

For the past several years relatives carrying pictures of disappeared persons would assemble outside the Supreme Court building, calling on the court to help recover them. Among them was the young wife of Naeem Noor Khan, a Pakistani computer expert who was a key link between the al Qaeda leadership hiding in the tribal areas and the worldwide terrorist network. Naeem was picked up in 2004 by Pakistani intelligence operatives, but he was freed by a Supreme Court order in early 2007, to the vexation of the Musharraf government and the United States.

In response, in March 2007 Musharraf summoned Chaudhry to his office and asked him to resign, accusing him of using his position for personal gain. He was placed under virtual confinement for several hours until a new chief justice took charge. A photo of a harassed chief justice surrounded by Musharraf's top generals that was released to the media triggered a countrywide protest by lawyers, who marched in the streets of Islamabad, Lahore, and Karachi. Within weeks the lawyers' demonstrations had evolved into a mass movement, with the protestors calling for fair elections, a civilian government, and the return of real democracy. The movement galvanized the major opposition parties, and Musharraf's hold on power grew tenuous. Amid this great unrest a major confrontation with the militant clerics of Islamabad's Lal Masjid who were affiliated with al Qaeda and both the Afghani and Pakistani Taliban leadership, was to prove a pivotal turning point in the fate of Musharraf's rule and the further escalation of militant violence, bringing it to the very heart of the country.

Tension was palpable inside the main hall of the mosque. A group of bearded men who squatted on the carpeted floor under the dome looked extremely anxious. Ceiling fans, whirling slowly, provided little relief from the suffocating heat on that summer afternoon. Masked gunmen took up position on the mosque's tall minarets, while others stood guard at the main gate. Hundreds of burka-clad young women kept vigil on the second floor of the adjoining seminary.

The leafy street outside was littered with broken glass, rocks, and burned-out vehicles, the remains of violence from that morning, when the neighborhood had become a battlefield. Barricaded inside the mosque, heavily armed militants had engaged in a fierce gun battle with paramilitary troops and the police. Dozens of people, including students of the mosque, members of the media, and paramilitary personnel, were killed or injured in the worst clashes ever witnessed in Pakistan's sleepy capital city, Islamabad.

Sporting his signature red skull cap, Abdul Rashid was constantly on his cell phone. His salt-and-pepper beard was unruly and his eyes were shrunken behind his round-framed glasses. In his late forties, the deputy head cleric of the Lal Masjid (Red Mosque) seemed anxious to get word about the military's movement. His older brother and the chief cleric,

Abdul Aziz, had already retired to his residential quarters, located at one end of the compound. A thin-framed, white-bearded man, Abdul Aziz had maintained a lower profile than his more charismatic sibling, but he was no less radical in his views. His fiery sermons attracted thousands of worshippers to the mosque's Friday prayers.

Established shortly after Pakistan's capital was moved from Karachi to the newly built Islamabad in 1965, Lal Masjid was named for its red walls and interiors. It had emerged as the center of religious activities attended by high government officials. But over the past several months Lal Masjid had served as the headquarters of the growing radical Islamist resistance to President Musharraf. Under the leadership of the two brothers, the Lal Masjid movement sought to take revolutionary action against a government that they regarded as an American puppet. The main objective, in the words of Abdul Rashid, was "to destroy the failed political system in Pakistan which has betrayed the majority of the country's poor" and to establish a Sharia state in its place.[12]

"Army troops are moving towards the mosque," Abdul Rashid told the men gathered in the main hall, dropping his phone. A deep silence fell. "How can we stop them?" one of them asked. "We will find some way," Abdul Rashid replied before the meeting broke up. It was July 3, 2007, the day the standoff between the militants of Lal Masjid and the government came to a head.[13]

Only a stone's throw from the headquarters of the ISI and a few blocks from the Parliament and the presidential palace, the mosque had become a base for Taliban-style vigilante squads. Led by fearsome, stick-wielding, burka-clad young women, in February 2007 radicals poured out of the mosque and the two madrassas, raiding houses allegedly used as brothels, kidnapping suspected prostitutes, and making bonfires of videocassettes and DVDs that they regarded as un-Islamic. The clerics set up courts to dispense their version of Islamic justice, and people began coming to them to resolve all sorts of grievances, from business matters to personal disputes. The clerics taunted the authorities to stop them. "The Islamic system takes action wherever the state fails," declared Abdul Rashid. "And in Pakistan the state has collapsed in all departments— from policing to jobs to morality. In all, it's only the elite who benefit." [14]

For months the administration had tolerated the activities of the self-styled vice squads, even after they kidnapped a number of policemen and ransacked government buildings. Their threats of holy war were ignored, and even a fatwa denouncing a female cabinet minister who had been photographed receiving a hug from a French skydiving instructor went unremarked. The Musharraf government hesitated to take action because the clerics had threatened to launch a wave of suicide attacks if any move were made against them.

The military also hesitated, surely due to its long ties with the mosque. For more than two decades Lal Masjid had harbored the rise of militant Islam under state patronage. It had been used for the recruitment and mobilization of volunteers to fight Pakistan's proxy war in Afghanistan and Kashmir, and the rupture of the long alliance between the military and the clerics had not come easily. The military had finally decided to act as the situation escalated to the point that some feared the militants might take over the capital city.

On the evening of July 3 troops backed by tanks and armored cars surrounded the sprawling complex of prayer halls, classrooms, and dormitories. The area was covered in complete darkness after the troops cut off electric and gas supply lines. Residents of adjoining villas fled as soldiers ringed the neighborhood with barbed wire and established a curfew.

Inside, the die-hard militants, many schooled in guerrilla warfare at mountain training camps in Kashmir and Afghanistan, positioned themselves behind concrete bunkers and sandbags. They were joined by the students of Jamia Fareedia, a radical madrassa attached to the mosque, as well as some four thousand students at the country's largest female Islamic seminary, known as Madrassa Hafza. Mostly in their teens, many of them were the children or relatives of militants killed fighting Pakistan's proxy war in Kashmir. They braced themselves for the impending confrontation, taking shelter in the basement, where they recited from the Quran and prayed for Allah's help.

The principal of the madrassa, a stout and graceful woman in her late thirties, Umme Hasan, consoled her pupils. Married to Abdul Aziz, she was known for her even more militant views; in fact she had mobilized the hundreds of young women who formed the nucleus of the Lal Masjid's movement for the enforcement of Sharia. They were taught to become wives of Mujahideen and produce the next generation of warriors to fight for the dominance of Islam. Umme Hasan often boasted that she had trained many girls to become suicide bombers.[15]

Suddenly the quiet of the night was broken by intermittent gunfire. The Pakistani Army's elite commando brigade had begun their assault, facing stiff resistance from the militants. As dusk fell the troops finally blew holes in the perimeter wall surrounding the mosque, as U.S.-made helicopter gunships hovered overhead and a barrage of mortars struck the compound. But the final onslaught was held off in order to allow time for the students to surrender. Announcements on loudspeakers warned the girls over and over again to leave the premises. Over the next few days the army set several deadlines for surrender and used a host of scare tactics, including warning explosions and bursts of gunfire, to weaken the resolve of the mosque's occupants. Many anxious parents waited outside for hours, calling their children on their cell phones and trying to persuade them to come out. Finally, as the deadline was extended, the girls started trickling out. Covered in black burkas they emerged one by one, silently weeping. Many of the male students also surrendered.

The resistance appeared to be collapsing by the night of July 4, when Abdul Aziz was caught by security forces trying to slip through the military cordon dressed in a burka and high heels. His failed attempt to flee gave some hope that the standoff would end without more bloodshed. In an interview broadcast on state television he asked his followers to give themselves up. He began the interview by lifting the black veil he was wearing to reveal a bushy white beard; smiling through much of the interview, he urged his followers to leave. But some of the women teachers had persuaded many of the girls to stay, and his younger brother was also resolute, vowing to fight to the end. Abdul Aziz's appeal also went unheeded by his wife, Umme Hasan, who had stayed behind with her young son. She told a local television network that she had no intention of giving herself up to the security forces. Despite his belated attempts to forge a resolution, Abdul Aziz was charged with twenty-five criminal offenses, including kidnapping, incitement to murder, and firearms offenses. His daughter, who had fled the mosque with him, was also taken into custody.

"We all are martyrs and those who are going to be martyred here would ask you on Judgment Day: are you responsible for the killing of our students?" Abdul Rashid proclaimed to the military via a call to a TV news station over his cell phone. "We all would ask you that: why did you kill us, for what sin?"[16]

On July 6 the military stepped up the shelling, blowing up

the entire compound wall, making way for troops to enter. Abdul Rashid was holed up in Madrassa Hafza with the remaining students. Their water and food were running out, and on the night of July 7 he made a dramatic turnaround, demanding safe passage. "I am ready to leave and settle in my village in Rohjan, if safe passage is given to me and my colleagues," he said in a telephone interview to a local TV channel.[17]

But Musharraf and his military commanders had toughened their stance after the deaths of soldiers in the siege, and safe passage was refused. Rashid was told to surrender and lay down his weapons unconditionally. At this point he became a virtual prisoner to the hard-liners in the mosque, who saw no hope of survival and refused to give themselves up.

On July 8 a desperate last-ditch attempt at compromise was made by some ruling party leaders, but both the military and the militants stuck to their positions. "The people inside the mosque should come out and surrender, otherwise I am saying it here, they risk being killed," Musharraf warned. His patience was fast running out.[18]

The parents of the students still inside the mosque made furious last attempts to convince their children to leave. Rahim Khan had traveled from the Mansehra district of the North West Frontier Province to get his daughter out of the mosque, but when after three days of trying to call her he was finally able to get through to her, she refused to come out. "I would prefer to die here than to leave my teachers," the fifteen-year-old Rizwana told him as he desperately tried to control his tears. "The teachers taught us about martyrdom and that it is a great achievement," she said before switching her phone off.[19]

On July 9 some students who had apparently been held against their will managed to escape, but many others remained. Abdul Rashid was reported to be holed up in a room with his elderly and ailing mother, who was too weak even to walk. She had decided to stay with her son.

For seven consecutive days the militants responded to the military's siege with automatic fire, showing little sign of fatigue or shortage of ammunition. Late in the evening of July 9 snipers positioned inside a minaret shot dead Lt. Col. Haroon Islam, the commander of the Special Forces leading the operation, and critically wounded two other officers as they tried to enter the complex through a broken wall. These killings vividly demonstrated how well trained the militants were.

The death of the commander was the last straw, and shortly thereafter Musharraf ordered the troops to prepare for a final assault. The military had been forced into a debacle of its own making.

Abdul Aziz and Abdul Rashid had learned their militancy from their father, Abdullah Ghazi, who has the head cleric of Lal Masjid during the war against the Soviets in Afghanistan and who had developed strong ties with the Islamist groups that joined in the fight. As was true for many clerics, he had received funding and guidance from the Pakistani military and intelligence agencies for recruiting militants to the cause, and Lal Masjid had become a citadel of militancy. After the Taliban's victory in Afghanistan, Abdullah Ghazi became closely associated with the movement and also with al Qaeda. In 1998 he traveled to Kandahar to pay homage to Mullah Omar, whom Pakistani radical Islamists regarded as their spiritual leader, and he took his younger son, Abdul Rashid, with him.

In his youth Abdul Rashid was a rebel and refused to follow the course charted for him by his father, who wanted his sons to become Islamic scholars. Abdul Aziz acquired religious training with extreme keenness and devotion, but Abdul Rashid took a different course, entering Quiad-e-Azam University in Islamabad, one of the country's most prestigious institutions, to study history. He wore Western clothes and refused to grow a beard. He received his master's degree in 1988, and a photo of him and his colleagues still hangs on the department's wall. According to one of his professors, "he was a normal, moderate student who was well adjusted to a co-educational system." [20] After leaving the university he joined UNESCO in Islamabad and also worked with the Ministry of Education. His work gave him an opportunity to travel to Europe, and he would proudly show a picture of himself in front of the Eiffel Tower. His Westernized lifestyle annoyed his father so much that he declared Abdul Aziz his sole heir.

But on a visit to Kandahar Abdul Rashid became radicalized, meeting Osama bin Laden as well as Mullah Omar. He met with bin Laden alone for an hour and discussed with him issues that had troubled him for a long time. "The meeting inspired me to work for the establishment of Islam," he said when he fondly narrated the story of the meeting.[21] At the end of the meeting, he recounted, he picked up bin Laden's glass of water and drank from it. An amused bin Laden asked him the reason for his action, to which Abdul Rashid replied, "I drank from your glass so that Allah would make me a warrior like you." [22]

In his first sermon at Friday prayers after his return to Islamabad, Abdullah Ghazi described his son's meeting with bin Laden in detail. "He is a great warrior of Islam and we Muslims should follow him," he told a spellbound gathering. He zealously started spreading the message.[23] Islamabad's most influential mosque became the main center for the propagation of Osama's call. When, just two months after Abdul Rashid's return from Kandahar, Abdullah Ghazi was assassinated inside the Lal Masjid compound, his death triggered unprecedented violence in the capital as thousands of madrassa students went on a rampage, engaging in pitched battle with security forces. Abdullah's murder remains unsolved, but suspicion has generally fallen on extremist Shia elements who were outraged by provocative sermons the Sunni cleric gave against their community.[24] Abdullah's murder propelled Abdul Rashid and his brother into leadership positions at the mosque and also pushed them further toward radicalism.

The long-standing links between the Pakistani military establishment and Lal Masjid turned hostile after President Musharraf allied himself with the United States following the 9/11 attacks. In his Friday sermon on September 13, 2001, Abdul Aziz declared to a packed gathering, "Allah has punished America for its anti-Islam policies and the sinful life of its population." At daily demonstrations in Islamabad Abdul Rashid also made passionate speeches defending Afghanistan against a U.S. invasion.[25] The mosque became the center of antigovernment protests. When Musharraf sent troops to Waziristan in 2004 Abdul Rashid led a campaign against the military operation and spearheaded a fatwa issued by a number of leading clerics, declaring the military action in Waziristan un-Islamic and proclaiming, "Those killed in the battle against Pakistani forces are martyrs."[26] The edict encouraged thousands of Islamists who had been reluctant to fight the Pakistani Army to join in the militant war in Waziristan.

The government retaliated by accusing Abdul Rashid of being involved in the plot to blow up Musharraf's convoy in Rawalpindi in December 2003, claiming that the explosives used in the attack had been stored in Lal Masjid. In 2004 Abdul Rashid went underground after the authorities displayed to the media an explosives-filled truck owned by the mosque as evidence of his involvement in terrorist activities. But a few months later he was cleared of the charges, apparently rescued by the federal minister for religious affairs, Ejaz ul Haq, the son of the late dictator, General Zia, and an old patron of Lal Masjid. Some reports suggested that Abdul Rashid was let off the hook under a secret deal in which he promised that he would no longer involve himself in political and antistate activities.[27]

The involvement in militant activities of the Lal Masjid and its affiliated madrassas increased substantially with the rise of the insurgency in the Pakistani tribal region. Seventy percent of the students of the seminaries attached to Lal Masjid came from the FATA territories and the North West Frontier Province, and Abdul Rashid had direct contact with the radical clerics and tribal leaders spearheading the insurgency.

The girls school at the mosque, Jamia Hafza, made headlines in 2005, when its students protested violently after Prime Minister Tony Blair of Great Britain called on Pakistan to crack down on radical Islamic schools in the wake of the July 7 London bombings that year. It was the first time Islamabad had witnessed the power of the Burka Brigade, as they became known, as thousands of stick-wielding girls fought the police.

In January 2007 the mosque was drawn into another controversy when a twelve-year-old Scottish girl, Molly Campbell, became the subject of a heated custody battle between her Scottish mother and Pakistani father. Barely four months after fleeing her mother's home in the Outer Hebrides, Molly, who was also known by her Islamic name, Misbah Rana, had come to live with her father in Pakistan and was admitted to the mosque's Hafza seminary. Molly said she did not want to stay with her mother because she was not Muslim. Late at night on January 10 I went to Lal Masjid to meet Molly after her mother, Louise, had given up the fight for her daughter's return, saying it had put too much of a strain on her health.

A black-turbaned man took me to Abdul Rashid's office inside the compound, where a number of gunmen were on security duty, some of them certainly not Pakistanis. It was quite evident to me from the presence of so many armed men inside the premises that the capital was sitting on a powder keg.

Abdul Rashid sat cross-legged on the carpeted floor with a Kalashnikov lying by his side. A young madrassa student worked on a computer in a corner. Abdul Rashid was fond of technology and a computer expert, and he had all the latest communication equipment installed on the premises. He established a data center with a number of computers, faxes, printers, and a scanner. To broadcast his speeches on the Internet he maintained his own website, and he monitored all incoming and outgoing calls through a digital computerized exchange. He also operated a pirate FM radio station out of the mosque.

Abdul Rashid went to the madrassa to get Molly, who arrived covered in a black burka. "I don't want to see my mother," she said to me. "She made me do things which I didn't want to do." It was clear to me that she was saying this under pressure.[28]

Tensions escalated further when, on January 21, burka-clad female students of the madrassa occupied an adjoining children's library, apparently protesting the demolition of mosques built illegally on state land. A few days later the Lal Masjid clerics presented a charter for proposed Islamic rule of the country, which envisaged a new social, political, and judicial system based on the Sharia, and on January 26, in his Friday sermon, Abdul Aziz called for the formation of revolutionary committees for the implementation of the charter.

In April the mosque announced the establishment of Sharia courts, which shortly thereafter caused a heated controversy by passing an edict against the tourism minister, Nilofer

Bakhtiar, for hugging a male parachuting instructor during her visit to France, calling for her to be fired. The edict ruined her political career, as she was forced to resign not only from the ministry, but also from the post of president of the women's wing of the ruling Pakistan Muslim League. The government had abdicated to the clerics' demands.

Musharraf was reluctant to crack down on the mosque after the clamor of discontent with his leadership in the wake of the lawyers' protests. In such a weakened state he feared the repercussions of moving on the clerics, but the government's inaction also reflected a split within the ranks. While some members of the government wanted to take a tough line against the Islamic groups gaining so much power, others, including several cabinet members, were openly sympathetic toward the jihadi groups, viewing them as valuable allies. They pushed for establishing a working relationship with those Islamic groups willing to talk. Most of the Islamic parties also supported the Lal Masjid's goal of Islamization of the Pakistani state and society, though few agreed with its tactics and many madrassa management boards de-affiliated themselves with the mosque.

The escalation of hostilities by the mosque clerics, as well as mounting pressure from the international community, finally forced Musharraf to order the siege. On July 1 he held a meeting of his top civil and military officials and declared, "There is no way we can tolerate these kinds of activities." [29]

Huge explosions rocked the city as Operation Silence unfolded on the dawn of July 10; this was the first time that Islamabad had witnessed such a ferocious battle right in the heart of the city. Some thirty women, including Umme Hasan and her daughter, Asma, came out soon after the commandos stormed

Madrassa Hafza. Most of the women appeared exhausted, and many complained of headaches as they were escorted out by the soldiers. As they boarded prison vehicles they chanted "Al-jihad, al-jihad!" Many students remained inside, and their relatives agonized about their fate. I talked to one parent, Maqsood Ahmed, who sat in the corner of a tent packed with parents praying for news of their children. He was an impoverished farmer from northern Pakistan, and he had been waiting for five days to be reunited with his twelve-year-old son.

By nightfall commandos had cleared the sprawling compound. Ninety-three people, including several soldiers, were killed in the siege.

On a visit a day later I found every part of the sprawling complex scarred by the battle. In the blackened basement where Abdul Rashid and half a dozen followers made a last stand, the wall had been shattered by explosives. The acrid stench of battle hung in the air. Metal furniture lay piled in a corner. The windowless room inside the girls madrassa was charred; a suicide bomber had detonated his charge as the commandos stormed the building. The people sheltering inside the room were so badly burned by the explosion that it was impossible to tell their gender or age. A severed head, presumed to be that of the suicide bomber, lay on the floor.

In the next room swarms of flies buzzed over the blood-stained floor and rubble was scattered where the militants had built a bunker. Walls that had been painted with Islamic verses were riddled with bullet holes, evidence of a vicious thirty-five-hour assault in which the commandos fought from room to room against heavily armed militants. "The resistance was beyond our expectations," said the commander who led the siege in an interview with the media that day at the mosque.

Inside the madrassa an inscription on a blackboard read, "O

God give us a martyr's death." Another inscription read, "Even if you are alone and your enemies are in their hundreds, do not see your weakness, but have faith in the Almighty."

The bare concrete rooms that served as classrooms and sleeping quarters were littered with broken glass and spent rifle cartridges. Books were piled into barricades, and the students' possessions lay scattered among upturned desks. Everywhere lay the remains of the militants' deadly arsenal: ammunition, machine-guns, rocket-propelled grenade launchers, antitank mines, unexploded suicide vests, and a crate of petrol bombs made from green Sprite bottles. Homemade bombs, gas masks, electronic scanners, and scores of jihadi DVDs lay alongside them.

The Lal Masjid itself was spared the worst of the fighting, but its entrance hall was destroyed by fire and chunks of masonry were blown from the minarets, which gunmen were said to have used as a vantage point. The speakers that were used to call the faithful to prayer hung from their wires, but the towering white dome appeared unscathed. Soldiers stood guard on the rubble, preventing the public from seeing the devastation. Almost seventy charred bodies were pulled from the debris and interred without ceremony in unmarked graves in Islamabad. A cleric read verses from the Quran, although full funeral rites were not observed. There were no names on the coffins, only numbered codes. Far from the destruction grieving relatives and villagers buried Abdul Rashid in his ancestral village of Rohjan in southern Punjab province amid chants of "Al-jihad, al-jihad."

The violent end of the Lal Masjid rebellion marked a critical watershed in Pakistan's struggle with Islamic militancy. It was the deadliest battle with militants since Musharraf declared his alliance with the United States, and al Qaeda leaders were quick to respond, calling for revenge. In an audio message posted on a website used by radical Islamists Osama bin Laden declared, "We in the al Qaeda organization call on God to witness that we will retaliate for the blood of . . . Abdul Rashid and those with him against Musharraf and those who help him, and for all the pure and innocent blood." [30] This was the first time bin Laden had urged Pakistanis "to fight against Musharraf, his army, his government and his supporters," and it was the ringing endorsement of the views of his deputy, Ayman al-Zawahiri, who argued that war should be waged first against the un-Islamic Muslim states, and then against the infidel armies. Until then bin Laden had avoided fomenting revolt within Islamic countries.

Zawahiri has since used the storming of the Lal Masjid as a rallying cry to fight the U.S.-backed Pakistani government and its military. "Let the Pakistani army know that the killing of Abdul Rashid and his students and the demolition of his mosque . . . have soaked the history of the Pakistani army in shame, which can only be washed away by retaliation," he declared in an audio message released soon after the assault. [31]

Abdul Rashid had predicted that any violent end to the siege would help speed an Islamic revolution in Pakistan. "We have a firm belief in God that our blood will lead to a revolution," he said in a statement issued three days before his death. "God willing, Islamic revolution will be the destiny of this nation." [32] His last words resonated powerfully in northwestern Pakistan, where tribal militant leaders now declared holy war against the government and the military.

On July 12 twenty thousand tribesmen, including hundreds of masked militants wielding assault rifles, demonstrated in the northwest region of Bajaur, chanting, "Death to Musharraf!" and "Death to America!" Across the country a rash of suicide bombings left hundreds of people dead. In a devastating suicide bombing on July 17 an army convoy in North Waziristan was blown up, killing twenty-four soldiers. The attack was the beginning of the most brutal wave of suicide bombings targeting security forces, not only in the northwest, but also in major Pakistani cities. More than eighty-eight bombings killed 1,188 people and wounded 3,209 in the first year following the Lal Masjid siege, an average of three people dying and more than seven people wounded every day from July 2007 to July 2008.[33]

The militant groups also ramped up their propaganda war, widely distributing video cassettes of Taliban killings and the speeches of their leaders, and militant spokesmen regularly appeared on national TV news channels claiming responsibility for the attacks. Scores of pirated FM radio transmitters operating from mosques across the tribal belt and part of the NWFP constantly exhorted people to jihad, and militant literature was circulated freely despite a government ban.

For the first time military and intelligence personnel and installations in high-security zones in cities such as Rawalpindi, Islamabad, and Lahore were targeted. On September 13, two months after the Lal Masjid siege, an eighteen-year-old boy blew himself up inside the high-security base of Zarrar Company, the elite commando unit of the Pakistan Army responsible for Operation Silence; twenty-two soldiers were killed. It was a major blow to the force, which had been specially trained by the United States to carry out counterterrorism operations. Because many believed that the attack would not have been possible without insider support, it seemed that the government now faced a well-coordinated guerrilla strategy that was being spearheaded by former army officers. One of the officers identified was Captain Khuram, who had been with Pakistan's Special Services Group and had also served in Zarrar Company. [34]

The Lal Masjid siege also spurred the loosely affiliated Pakistani Taliban groups into forming an official alliance. This was another major turning point in the rise of the insurgency.

CHAPTER 5

Operation Earthquake

As the Pakistani Interior Ministry report issued in early 2007 stressed, the clerics of Lal Masjid mosque had formed strong ties with militant leaders, particularly with Baitullah Mehsud in South Waziristan and Mullah Fazlullah in the Swat Valley. In addition hundreds of students at the two madrassas affiliated with the mosque were from the Swat Valley and districts of South Waziristan under Baitullah's dominance. Both militant leaders reacted swiftly and brutally to the raid on the mosque.

On July 12, 2007, in one of his radio addresses, Fazlullah declared jihad against the government, vowing to avenge the death of Abdul Rashid; just a few days later a military convoy moving toward the Swat was attacked and thirteen soldiers were killed. A spate of suicide attacks and roadside bombings in the following weeks killed dozens more soldiers.

Baitullah officially pulled out from the peace deal he had made with the government in February 2005, justifying the move by claiming that the military had deployed troops in his area in violation of the agreement. Fierce fighting resumed, and on August 30 Baitullah scored a huge victory when his men captured 260 soldiers, seventeen trucks, and a huge cache of arms in a spectacular attack on an army convoy near the

Laddah military fort, just twenty-five miles from the regional headquarters at Wana. The troops, including nine officers, surrendered without firing a shot, causing great embarrassment to the military leadership.[1]

By seizing such a large number of troops, Baitullah was displaying his growing power, to impressive effect. The incident was the biggest blow for the Pakistani military since the start of the offensive in the tribal areas in 2004, and had a powerfully demoralizing effect on the security forces. Hundreds of paramilitary soldiers from the surrounding regions began surrendering their weapons to Baitullah's forces; they felt little motivation to fight after so many regular army soldiers had given themselves up so readily.

Adding to the humiliation Baitullah paraded the commanding officer in charge of the convoy, Lieutenant Colonel Zafar, and two other officers before the international media after they had been in detention for more than a month. They appeared physically weakened and demoralized but were forced to say that they were being treated well. They did not know that three of their colleagues had already been killed by the militants to put pressure on the government to accept Baitullah's demands. In negotiating for the soldiers' lives Baitullah was stipulating that the military withdraw from South Waziristan and release thirty militants who had been captured, and he had ordered the beheading of three hostages to show that he meant business. Negotiations dragged on for week after week, making the government appear utterly powerless before the militant threat.

In trying to negotiate with Baitullah the government was blatantly denying the reality of his power and intent. He continued to launch attacks, and a UN report released in September 2007 blamed him for almost 80 percent of the suicide bombings carried out in Afghanistan at that time.[2]

Public anger at the Musharraf government swelled as the presidential elections, to be held on October 6, approached. The president tried to clamp down on the media, shutting down several antigovernment private TV channels, but he received a serious blow when, on July 20, the Supreme Court reinstated Iftikhar Mohammed Chaudhry to his position as chief justice, throwing out the presidential order dismissing him. Musharraf now faced a hostile judiciary as he decided to stand for a second term as president, in violation of the country's constitution, which barred a serving officer from holding any elected office. He had given himself what he called a one-time waiver in the previous election, and was now going against his prior commitment not to extend his hold over both offices. The widespread protests of his violation of the constitution continued to gain force, and the Supreme Court was set to rule on the legitimacy of his standing in the election. There was no way that Chaudhry would grant legitimacy to the person who had humiliated him. Musharraf's political future clearly hung in the balance. With some government ministers openly criticizing his policies, he faced intense pressure to step down.

In a desperate attempt to shore up his hold on power, Musharraf reached out to an old adversary, Benazir Bhutto. This was not the first time he had made the effort to make an alliance with her. He had solicited her support back in August 2006, when he was running into stiff opposition in the National Assembly to the passage of a women's bill of rights. In an unexpected telephone call from his office in Rawalpindi he told her, "It is time the moderate political forces unite,"[3] and he asked for her support of the bill. Until then he had insisted that there was no place for her in Pakistani politics. This was the first direct contact between the two leaders since Musharraf seized power in October 1999 and was the culmination of protracted secret negotiations between aides to Bhutto and Musharraf. Bhutto agreed to lend her support, and the bill was passed by the National Assembly on November 15, 2006. The way was paved for continued negotiations on a deal that would allow Bhutto to return to the country and take part in the next parliamentary elections in a power-sharing deal with Musharraf.

Strained as their relations were, a degree of alliance between them made a certain sense. Bhutto was the only major opposition political figure in the country who had supported Musharraf's alliance with the United States; in fact she had often criticized the government for not being fully enough on board with Washington. In lectures in America and in interviews with the Western media she had often accused Musharraf of playing a double game. She promised to allow U.S. forces to move into Pakistan's tribal regions if she returned to power.

In the face of the growing opposition to Musharraf, and in consideration of Bhutto's pro-West position, the Bush administration had been working to facilitate the negotiations between her and Musharraf, though Washington was still highly skeptical of Bhutto. The host of corruption charges against her, as well as her prior ineptitude in running the government, remained matters of serious concern. But the administration also realized that by this time Bhutto's support was essential for Musharraf to be able to hold on to power for another term, and the specter of a right-wing takeover of the government compelled the administration to push for the deal between them. Bhutto was now vigorously courted by the U.S. State Department, whose officials had previously refused to take her telephone calls, and eventually Secretary of State Condoleezza Rice got directly involved in the talks.

Bhutto appeared to believe that the United States sincerely

supported the struggle for the restoration of democracy in Pakistan, and she made it clear that she was willing to share power with Musharraf under certain conditions: that he step down as army chief; that a bar on her assuming a third term as prime minister be removed; that international watch groups be allowed to monitor the election; and that Musharraf withdraw the long-standing corruption charges against her and her husband, Asif Ali Zardari.

On January 27, 2007, Bhutto arrived in Abu Dhabi for a secret face-to-face talk with Musharraf. They had last met in 1994, during her second term as prime minister, and the meeting had not been pleasant. Musharraf was then director general of military operations, and he had briefed her about a military plan to occupy some Indian posts in the Kargil Mountains in the disputed region of Kashmir, the intention being to apply pressure to the Indian forces there. Bhutto rejected the proposal, which she believed might lead to a wider military conflict between the two countries. This was the operation that Musharraf had ordered as the army chief five years later, which had set in motion the events that led to his coup. Even before that 1994 meeting Musharraf had felt strong antipathy toward the Bhutto family. Back in the early 1970s his father, who was an employee of the Pakistani Foreign Office, was sacked by the government of Zulfikar Ali Bhutto, and Musharraf had never forgotten his father's humiliation.

Bhutto was uncertain about how productive talking to Musharraf would be, but to her surprise, she was to say later, he was forthcoming and candid, willing to discuss all the contentious issues between them. He reportedly not only agreed to step down as army chief, but also conceded to her other demands, including that all charges against her husband be dropped. However, these concessions came at a price: Musharraf required that she not return to Pakistan before the elections, and she reluctantly agreed. The meeting ended on a pleasant note, with Musharraf accepting Bhutto's invitation to attend a New Year's function at her house in Karachi.[4] Bhutto was confident the Pakistan People's Party would sweep the polls in the general election scheduled for January 2008, giving the party the majority in Parliament, which would then name her prime minister.[5]

Musharraf was clearly not serious about fulfilling his pledge to step down as army chief, however, as he also indicated that his decision about whether or not he would dismiss the corruption charges against her and her husband would be delayed until after the presidential election.

After Musharraf faced intensified opposition in the wake of his firing of the chief justice, he and Bhutto met again, in Abu Dhabi, in July 2007. With Musharraf's hold on power substantially weakened, this meeting took a different tone. Bhutto pushed for the implementation of the promises Musharraf had made in the January meeting, particularly dropping all the charges against her and Zardari, which the United States was also pressuring him to do. Within a few days of the meeting some of Bhutto's frozen funds were released, but the corruption charges were still not dropped.

As the summer proceeded a plan took shape through discussions in Islamabad, Washington, and London. The goal was to bring democratic legitimacy to the Pakistani government, but without opening the door to forces that would threaten the alliance with the United States. Reaching this goal involved a number of steps: Musharraf was to win reelection as president in the fall, arrange for Bhutto to return from exile, and step down from his position as head of the military. As Bhutto had planned, her party would win a majority in the parliamentary elections in January 2008, making her prime minister, and the two would collaborate in pursuing a pro-American, anti-Islamic extremist agenda.

Well aware of Musharraf's growing weakness, in August Bhutto summoned her senior party leaders to New York to discuss the future course of action, and she threatened to pull out of the talks if Musharraf did not immediately concede to her demands.[6] She now wanted to return to the country before the elections. The two engaged in many long, late-night phone conversations, with Condoleezza Rice and her deputy, Richard Boucher, pushing them to firm up a deal. On September 1, 2007, Bhutto upped the ante, declaring that she was returning to Pakistan "very soon," regardless of whether or not she had reached a power-sharing agreement with Musharraf, which finally sealed the deal. On October 5, just a day before the presidential elections, Musharraf signed the National Reconciliation Ordinance, giving amnesty against all charges to Bhutto and her husband, as well as other political leaders, including former premier Nawaz Sharif. In return Bhutto and the PPP agreed not to boycott the presidential elections.

The legitimacy of the elections was challenged nonetheless when all of the other opposition parties quit the Parliament in protest. The Supreme Court allowed the elections to take place on time, but indicated that it would rule afterward on the legitimacy of Musharraf's candidacy. The elections took place amid heightened security, with Islamabad's Constitution Avenue, where the Parliament and the presidential palaces are located, barricaded with barbed wire and armored cars. Paramilitary and military troops patrolled the streets of the city, and protesters clashed with riot police not only in the capital but also in other major cities. With the opposition boycotting the elections, Musharraf garnered 671 of the total 684 votes polled by the Electoral College, but the future of his government remained undecided, pending the Supreme Court's decision on his eligibility.

Musharraf had clung to power, but the hold was quite tenuous, and he was to face ever more heated opposition even as the attacks by militants against the military continued to rage out of control and more and more suicide bombings terrorized the population, spreading into the major cities.. Fighting intensified in North Waziristan, where forty-five soldiers were killed during three days of clashes, from October 6 to 9.

On October 9 the pressure on Musharraf mounted further when the White House released a national strategy for combating terrorism, calling Pakistan an al Qaeda safe haven. This was the first time that the country had been designated as such in a White House policy document. "Al Qaeda has protected its top leadership, replenished operational lieutenants, and regenerated a safe haven in Pakistan's Federally Administered Tribal Areas, FATA—core capabilities that would help facilitate another attack," the statement read.[7]

Later in October Musharraf ordered ten thousand troops into the Swat Valley in the first major operation against Fazlullah and his forces. Within weeks, the troops cleared most of the areas, pushing the militants into the mountains. Hundreds of militants were killed and many senior commanders of Fazlullah were captured, but Fazlullah and a large number of his forces retreated into the surrounding mountains. This was not the last that would be seen of them in the Swat. The Supreme Court had yet to rule on the legitimacy of the election results, but with protests mounting it was becoming clear that Chief Justice Chaudhry would eventually rule to annul them. In a desperate move to preempt that ruling and retain power, on November 3 Musharraf declared a state of emergency across the country and once again sacked the chief justice, accusing him of conspiring to unseat him. The move provoked strong condemnation from his Western allies and triggered howls of protest within the country.

During all of this chaos negotiations with Baitullah Mehsud over the soldiers he had taken captive continued to drag on, until finally they were released on November 4. But their release was secured only because the government had accepted all of Baitullah's demands. Encouraged by the triumph, Baitullah's men shortly after launched a series of lightning strikes on army forts throughout the area, and in December, to avenge the humiliation, the army launched its biggest offensive since 2004. The three-pronged ground operation backed by air force jets was code-named Earthquake, and it devastated the parts of South Waziristan under Baitullah's control.

Villages along the road to Laddah were turned into piles of bricks and twisted iron, scorched by the bombing. The view from army helicopters was chilling: clusters of mud homes, nestled in pockets of forest at the foot of stark, jagged mountains, with not a soul in sight. The fighting forced some 200,000 people to flee their homes, leaving behind their herds and crops, unattended.

I visited a devastated structure of a building, apparently used to train suicide bombers, in the center of Kotkai village. The literature and computers and other equipment seized from the destroyed compound revealed details of the training process. A video showed a classroom where ten- to twelve-year-olds were sitting in formation, with white bands inscribed with Quranic verses wrapped around their forehead. They were shown videos of destruction from U.S. drone attacks in the tribal regions and of the killing of civilians in Afghanistan by bombing from NATO jets, and they were taught how to handle weapons and how to make and detonate improvised explosive devices and prepare suicide jackets and were trained in ambush tactics.

Almost 90 percent of the suicide bombers in Pakistan have been between twelve and eighteen.[8] Not only were young children generally less suspect than adults would be, and therefore easily able to reach their targets unnoticed, but they were easily brainwashed, taught that sacrificing oneself was a "ticket to Paradise." Their poverty also made them ripe targets for the jihadi cause. Baitullah had turned training in suicide bombing into a mass-production affair. In 2008, during a meeting with a group of journalists, he boasted that suicide bombers were his atom bombs in the battle against infidels, and his bombers were blamed for the majority of the attacks all around the country.[9]

The training center in Kotkai was run by one of the most ferocious Pakistani Taliban commanders. Qari Hussain had often boasted that through his lectures he could convince anyone to become a suicide bomber in ten minutes. A tall and charismatic man in his thirties, Hussain was trained in al Qaeda camps in Afghanistan and was reputed to be a fierce fighter. He had received religious training in a madrassa in Karachi before returning to his home in South Waziristan to join Baitullah, where he was also associated with Lashkar-e-Jhangvi, a radical Sunni sectarian group closely linked to al Qaeda. Pakistani military officials were confident that Hussain had been killed in the bombing of Kotkai, but a few days later he mocked the reports of his death at a press conference held at a government school building in South Waziristan. "I am alive, don't you see me?" he taunted.[10]

Many of the boys in the camp had close relatives who had been killed in the Pakistani military's operations against the militants, and the tribal code of honor required them to avenge the death of their dear ones. The number of such volunteers had swelled with the escalation in fighting, and it was discovered that a large number of recruits to the many different training centers came from the poverty-stricken southern part of Punjab, which had long been the stronghold of militant and Sunni sectarian groups. They were recruited mostly from radical madrassas, their number increasing especially after the storming of Lal Masjid.

In many cases the young boys were taken away without their parents' knowledge. Parents would send them to madrassas thinking that they were getting an education and, more important, free food, and instead they were turned into jihadi fighters. Parents weren't informed of where their children had been taken. "We did not have any clue as to where he went," one such father recounted to me. "I was horrified when I was told that my son could have been a suicide bomber." [11]

In 2008 I interviewed a number of children who had been trained to become suicide bombers; they had been picked up in military raids. Wearing dirty clothes and broken sandals, the boys looked haggard. Some of them fidgeted nervously with their soiled white skullcaps as they spoke about their ordeals at the training camps. "It was very tough there. Occasionally we had to train sixteen hours a day," said Abdul Wahab in a choked voice. "I was told that it was the religious duty of every Muslim to secure training to fight the enemies of Islam." He panicked when, a few days after he arrived at the camp, he was told that he was to become a suicide bomber.

Murad Ali, age thirteen, was in fifth grade in a school in Mingora when he was taken to a camp in Chuprial, a mountainous region in Swat. At first he was thrilled when he was given a gun to fire, but his excitement vanished when he was informed about the next stage of his training. "My instructor told me that martyrdom earned the greatest reward from Allah," said Ali, who had still not recovered from the shock.

The boys recounted that those ready to go on suicide missions would be separated from other trainees, and they were not allowed to have any contact with their family members or friends. They were told to spend all of their time in the days before an attack praying or reading religious literature. On the appointed day a bomber-to-be would be taken to a mosque, where he would be congratulated for being chosen by God to become a martyr. Sometimes he would be heavily drugged before being sent on his mission. The bombers were under strict instructions not to allow anyone, not even their parents, to stand in the way of jihad. "You must not even hesitate to kill your parents if they are on the wrong side," said Khurshid Khan, age fourteen, who had been selected for advanced training in one of Baitullah's camps in South Waziristan.[12]

Once trained, the children might also be sold to other groups. "A young trained boy can fetch thousands of rupees," said a Pakistani official. Many children trained at Qari Hussain's camp had been sold to other groups. The going price for child bombers was $7,000 to $14,000—huge sums in Pakistan, where the per capita income is about $2,600 a year. The price depended on how quickly the bomber was needed and how close the child was expected to get to the target.

A chilling revelation about the ruthless exploitation of children came to light when investigations found that one young boy was bought from Waziristan to kill a rival political leader. The teenage tribal boy detonated himself when Rashid Akbar Niwani, a member of Parliament, was meeting his supporters in his hometown of Bhakar in northeastern Pakistan in October 2008. Niwani escaped unhurt, but twenty-two of his supporters were killed.

The escalating number of suicide bombings unleashed around the country, even as the military renewed its efforts to crack down on the militants, fueled not only intense fear among the public but increasing outrage at the military. The devastation wreaked by the military in the towns also intensified resentment. Houses were demolished as a form of collective punishment on the tribe for providing shelter to the militants, which was greatly resented, especially as many of the locals argued that they had been forced to support the Taliban under the threat of being beheaded.[13] Many of these tribesmen had actively been supporting the militants and even harbored them, but others had supported the Taliban only out of fear.

The objective of Operation Earthquake was to wrest control of the area from Baitullah and force him to accept peace on the government's terms. The operation did put pressure on Baitullah, but it failed to drive him out of the area. Most of his forces simply moved into the nearby mountains, to return later, and the operation had no limiting effect on suicide bombings. Not only was Baitullah's power not seriously impaired, but he was now to be instrumental in bringing about a more closely coordinated alliance of the various Pakistani Taliban groups.

Until the siege of Lal Masjid, the Taliban groups had operated independently of each other in their own regions. The storming of the mosque and subsequent military operations inspired them to unite. On December 14, 2007, some forty militant leaders, commanding forty thousand militant fighters, gathered in South Waziristan to form a united front under the banner of Tehrik-e-Taliban Pakistan. They unanimously elected Baitullah Mehsud their emir, the supreme leader of the new organization.

Prominent among those attending were Hafiz Gul Bahadur from North Waziristan, Malwi Nazir from South Waziristan, Faqir Mohammed from Bajaur, and Fazlullah from Swat. The presence of Gul Bahadur and Malwi Nazir, both belonging to the Wazir tribe, was especially notable because they both had a long-standing rivalry with Baitullah.[14] The Shura, or central council, that was set up at this meeting included representatives from all the seven tribal regions as well as parts of the NWFP, including Swat, Malakand Buner, and Dera Ismail Khan, where the Taliban movement was active. The council passed an eight-point charter calling for the enforcement of Islamic Sharia rule in the country and vowing to continue fighting against NATO forces in Afghanistan and against the Pakistani military. The council also gave a ten-day deadline to the government to stop military operations in Swat and the tribal areas or it would unleash attacks in the provincial capital of Peshawar. The turmoil overtaking the country was to be ratcheted up even further just weeks later, with the most shocking suicide attack yet.

Benazir Bhutto had returned to Pakistan on October 18, 2007, to a tumultuous welcome. She traveled immediately to the mausoleum of Mohammed Ali Jinnah, Pakistan's founder, where she planned to give a speech. The government had taken unprecedented security measures to protect her. About twenty thousand security personnel lined the route, and sophisticated antibomb jamming devices were fitted to her vehicle. Mobile phone signals were blocked in the area, and armed bodyguards accompanied her truck. The rooftop of her truck had been fitted with a bullet-proof enclosure, but she spent most of the day standing at the front of the vehicle, chatting with party officials and waving to the crowd.

Suddenly, in quick succession, two huge blasts struck her truck. Hundreds of her supporters had run toward the vehicle after the first blast, only to be caught in the second explosion. Bhutto had just stepped inside the truck to use the bathroom when the blasts took place. Mayhem ensued, with mutilated bodies littering the street, while people shouted for help. More than 140 people were killed, making this the worst terrorist attack in the nation's history. Many of the dead were policemen and Bhutto's personal security guards, who had formed a moving security cordon around the vehicle. Bhutto survived.

Security had been a major concern for Bhutto as she finalized the preparations for her homecoming. U.S. officials were in constant touch with Musharraf to discuss security arrangements, and though Musharraf was not happy with her decision to return before the elections, he assured the Americans that he would protect her. He had also warned her, though, "Your security is based on the state of our relationship." [15]

Not fully satisfied with Musharraf's assurances, Bhutto went to Washington to lobby officials and lawmakers, believing that only the U.S. government could guarantee her safe return. Everything would work out if they were behind her, she believed.[16] She called on Senator John Kerry, who chaired the powerful Senate Foreign Relations Committee, to press her request that the United States guarantee her safety, but he could offer no such guarantee.[17] She then proposed that Vice President Dick Cheney call Musharraf to request full protection for her, but that phone call was never made.[18]

Musharraf continued to try to persuade her to postpone her return until the last moment, when she boarded a chartered Emirate Airlines flight from Dubai to Karachi on the morning of October 18, 2007. She certainly had Washington's blessings, but she was well aware of the risk to her life. In an interview with Wolf Blitzer of CNN on September 28 she talked about the possibility of an attack on herself and said she was also considering hiring a foreign security firm.[19] She called the U.S. ambassador in Islamabad, Anne Paterson, when she landed at

Karachi Airport, complaining about the insufficient security, and the ambassador relayed Bhutto's concerns to Musharraf.

After the bombing on October 18, Bhutto blamed Brig. Ejaz Shah, the chief of the Intelligence Bureau, and the chief ministers of the Sindh and Punjab provinces of plotting the attack. Certainly the attack was expertly planned. The investigation revealed that the suicide bomber, who was believed to be in his early twenties, had used powerful plastic explosives. Bhutto claimed that she had warned the Pakistani government that suicide bomb squads would target her upon her return, and that the government had failed to act, though she was careful not to blame Musharraf himself for the attacks. Instead she accused "certain individuals within the government who abuse their positions, who abuse their powers" to advance the cause of Islamic militants.[20] In particular she accused the ISI of hiring the services of a veteran militant commander, Qari Saifullah Akhtar, to target her procession. He had been the leader of Harkat-ul-Jihad al Islami, a pro–al Qaeda group also closely linked with the Taliban. Bhutto had asserted in her book *Reconciliation* that Akhtar was involved in a failed coup attempt against her by Islamist military officers in 1995: "It was Qari whom the intelligence officials in Lahore turned to for help before my homecoming on October 18, 2007."[21] Akhtar has denied the accusation.

Though the question of who had carried out the attack was to remain a mystery, there was no doubt that it had the hallmarks of attacks perpetrated by militants linked to al Qaeda. Bhutto had first become a target of the Taliban after she suggested that she would help U.S. troops hunt for Osama bin Laden and other al Qaeda figures inside Pakistan. She further evoked the ire of the militants for supporting the raid on the Lal Masjid. "I'm glad there was no cease-fire with the militants in the mosque because cease-fires simply embolden the militants," she told Britain's Sky TV. "There will be a backlash, but at some time we have to stop appeasing the militants."[22] She was the only opposition leader to speak out against the militants.

On the day before her arrival the Taliban had publicly threatened to kill her. "We will carry out attacks on Benazir Bhutto as we did on General Musharraf," Haji Omar, a Taliban spokesman, declared.[23] Pakistani and some foreign intelligence reports warned that at least three groups with al Qaeda or Taliban links were plotting suicide attacks. Bhutto also expressed fear that retired military officials were plotting her assassination. Taliban commanders were "just pawns," she said. "It is those forces behind [them] that have presided over the rise of extremism and militancy in my country." Hours before the attack she reiterated those concerns: "I know who these people are, I know the forces behind them, and I have written to Gen. Musharraf about this."[24]

Bhutto was on a short trip to Dubai when Musharraf declared a state of emergency on November 3. She returned to Karachi the same evening and contacted a Musharraf aide. He explained to her the reason for Musharraf's radical measure and promised to lift the state of emergency within a couple of weeks, but Bhutto was unconvinced.[25]

The next day she pulled out of the deal with Musharraf and threatened to lead nationwide protests. While acknowledging that Pakistan faced a political crisis, she noted that Musharraf's declaration of a state of emergency, unless lifted, would make it very difficult to have fair elections, and she added, "The extremists need a dictatorship, and dictatorship needs extremists."[26] She was briefly put under house detention when she tried to hold a protest rally in Islamabad and Lahore.

In mid-November President Bush dispatched Deputy Secretary of State John Negroponte to Pakistan to put the agreement between Bhutto and Musharraf back on track.

Washington also wanted Musharraf to end the state of emergency immediately and take off his uniform before the parliamentary elections. He agreed to both requests, becoming a civilian president.

Amid this turmoil, on November 25, 2007, Nawaz Sharif also returned to the country, ending seven years of exile. Just months earlier he had been forcibly sent back to Saudi Arabia after he landed at Islamabad, but Musharraf could not stop him this time. He flew to his hometown, Lahore. In a last-ditch attempt to stop Sharif's return Musharraf had flown to Riyadh to meet King Abdullah, requesting that he not allow the former prime minister to leave the country, but Musharraf was left with no options after the Saudi monarch refused to prevent Sharif from returning home.[27] Sharif's return further heated up the political temperature in the country.

Musharraf handed over the army command to Gen. Ashfaq Kayani on December 3, bringing an end to his forty-six-year military career. "I will no longer command . . . but my heart and my mind will always be with you," he told his officers, trying to hold back tears.[28] He was certainly not happy to hang up his uniform, which he had often described as his second skin. Though he tried to convince himself and his allies that the army leadership would stand by him, when the call later came for him to step down from the presidency even his loyalists in the army were not there to support him.

As the campaign for the parliamentary elections proceeded, Bhutto was warned repeatedly about the danger of further attacks, but she often ignored the warnings. Just ten days after the founding of the militant coalition Tehrik-e-Taliban Pakistan, on December 27, 2007, a second attack on Bhutto succeeded. A suicide bomber blew himself up after firing gunshots at her as she came out of an election rally in Rawalpindi, close to Pakistani Army headquarters.

Minutes earlier Bhutto had addressed an election rally in which thousands of her party supporters converged at a sprawling park right in the heart of Rawalpindi. "We will defeat the forces of extremism and militancy with the power of the people," she vowed, speaking passionately about the destruction wrought by the Taliban militants. Her head covered with her signature white scarf, she held the crowd in thrall, alluding to the death threats she faced. "I put my life in danger and came here because I feel this country is in danger. People are worried. We will bring the country out of this crisis," she told the crowd. She left the rally confident of her victory in the election.

As her bullet-proof sport utility vehicle moved slowly through a crowd of jostling supporters, she again ignored security advice and suddenly popped her head through the vehicle's sunroof. The crowd shouted and cheered as she waved, and then a pistol shot rang out, followed by a massive explosion. She tried to duck back into the vehicle, but the shock wave from the blast knocked her head into a lever attached to the sunroof, fracturing her skull. She was dead a few minutes later, the highest profile victim yet of the terrorism she had vowed to fight.

In less than twenty-four hours the government released an intercepted message between Baitullah Mehsud and his supporters in which the Taliban leader praised the killing and, according to the officials, appeared to take credit for it. The authenticity of the intercept was, however, questioned by Bhutto's supporters, who suspected a deeper conspiracy behind the assassination. Many voiced suspicion that Musharraf's government had played a role in Bhutto's assassination, alleging the involvement of intelligence officials.

A UN commission accused the Musharraf government of failing to protect Bhutto. In a scathing report issued on April

16, 2010, the three-member investigative panel concluded that the suicide bombing that killed her could have been prevented and that police deliberately failed to pursue an effective investigation into the killings. "No one believes that this boy acted alone," the report stated. "A range of government officials failed profoundly in their efforts first to protect Ms. Bhutto, and second to investigate with vigor all those responsible for her murder, not only in the execution of the attack, but also in its conception, planning and financing." [29]

Bhutto's death raised a host of troubling questions about the future direction of Pakistani politics and society. Never in Pakistan's history had a political tragedy had such a deep impact: a country so divided was united in its grief for the unrivaled leader of Pakistan's most respected political dynasty. But this fleeting unity betrayed a vulnerability that reflected the reality of a leaderless nation.

Ultimately Bhutto's death further widened the divide in the country. The tragedy revived the wounds caused by the execution of her father thirty years earlier and heightened fears that the government and the military had lost control of the country.

In the months that followed, the newly organized Taliban movement swept across the entire northwestern region of Pakistan, extending to the Bajaur and Mohmand tribal regions, which, unlike the remote reaches of Waziristan, bordered the major population centers of the NWFP, spreading fear that the Taliban would gain control of the main arteries that connected that province to other parts of the country. Bajaur now became a central hub from which the militants launched attacks. The political turmoil in the country was facilitating the relentless growth of what was evolving into a coordinated insurgency aimed at taking charge of the Pakistani state as the Taliban had taken over Afghanistan.

CHAPTER 6

Turning the Tide

Benazir Bhutto's tragic assassination catapulted her husband, Asif Ali Zardari, to the center of Pakistani politics.
He returned to the country only a few hours after her assassination and took up the leadership of the Pakistan People's
Party. His ascent to the position was ironic, as Bhutto had
said she did not want him to return to politics. "He will not
have any role in politics," she was quoted telling close aides
and friends.[1] Relations between her and Zardari had become
estranged over the years, and after his release from jail in 2004
he moved to New York, where he chose to live a life of his
own, away from his wife and children. But in the face of criticism of his assumption of the role, and to the utter surprise
of her supporters and friends, Zardari produced Bhutto's will,
which declared that he should lead the party in the event she
was killed. Many of her friends and associates believed the will
was fabricated, but given the turmoil in the party due to her
death, he faced little opposition in the party ranks.[2]

   In the parliamentary elections, which were moved to February in the wake of Bhutto's assassination, the PPP swept
the polls in a sympathy vote, returning to power after twelve
years. To the surprise of many, Zardari proved to be a shrewd
political operator, quickly building a coalition of all the major

political parties in the country, with the explicit aim of forcing Musharraf, who was now a lame duck, out of the presidency. The new army chief, Gen. Ashfaq Kayani, was not keen to prop up Musharraf any longer, as the military faced increasing criticism for providing protection to him. His days in office were clearly numbered, but Musharraf refused to concede for several more months.

In June Zardari sent the national security advisor, Mahmood Ali Durrani, a retired general who had a long-standing relationship with Musharraf, to ask Musharraf to step down. But Musharraf reacted with fury, telling Durrani, "There is no question of my stepping down."[3] When the Bush administration conveyed its strong desire that Musharraf work out an exit plan, Musharraf tried to convince the Americans that he was indispensable and could weather the crisis. As the political forces rallied against him and prepared to vote on impeachment, in August 2008 General Kayani finally directly conveyed to his former chief the concern of his commanders about the untenability of the situation, and Musharraf realized he was left with no option. In a long and emotional televised speech on August 18, 2008, he announced his resignation.

Zardari had set his sights on the presidency, having indicated to U.S. officials long before Musharraf's exit his intention to take up the top job. Though officially the United States remained neutral in the campaign that soon followed, it was apparent that Zardari had the Bush administration's blessing, in part because the administration believed that Zardari would be a cooperative ally and more pliable than his wife. He also had a strong proponent in Anne Paterson, the U.S. ambassador to Pakistan. But though the corruption charges against him in Pakistan had been dropped as part of the power-sharing deal between Musharraf and Bhutto, he still faced money-laundering charges in Switzerland, an embarrassment that might serve as an impediment to his election. Those charges too were finally dropped after the new PPP government asked the Swiss government to stop the judicial proceedings; U.S. officials reportedly played a significant role in those negotiations. At the same time the Swiss released $60 million from Zardari's Swiss bank accounts, which had been frozen since the late 1990s.[4]

Though American support was surely important in Zardari's victory in the election, his success was also due to the deftness with which he had shored up a coalition of political parties in support of his presidency. Still, his election to the country's highest office came as a shock to even Bhutto's most ardent supporters, who blamed him for the failure of her two governments. His rating at the opinion polls was less than 20 percent at the time of the elections, and the return of his $60 million just a few days before the elections further destroyed whatever little credibility he had. Nonetheless he had prevailed.

Zardari's ascendency was yet another swing of the pendulum by which control of the government had arced for so many years between military rule and civilian governments dogged by allegations of corruption, and he has remained highly controversial. Widespread allegations contend that he has turned the country into a personal fiefdom, with cronies running the affairs of state, and he has failed to give sustained attention to the critical problem of the militant threat. As the Bush administration expected, he has, however, been a reliable ally in stepped-up efforts by the United States to crack down on al Qaeda leaders in the Pakistani territories, giving his support to increased drone operations that have resulted in a string of killings of high-level operatives. Those strikes have also caused increasing anger among the Pakistani public and intense hostility toward Zardari, who is widely perceived to be a stooge of the Americans.

Even before Zardari's election, Washington had determined that it must take more vigorous action in the tribal territories, and in July 2008 President Bush passed a secret order authorizing raids inside Pakistan without the prior approval of Islamabad. The order also approved carrying out ground assaults by U.S. Special Operations forces to kill or capture al Qaeda operatives. The order clearly illustrated a lack of faith in Pakistan's ability and will to combat the militants, and probably also reflected suspicions that the Pakistani intelligence agencies were not fully trustworthy. U.S. security officials had often accused Pakistani intelligence agents of alerting militants in advance of strikes.[5] The political unrest that had been roiling the country was also a strong factor in the administration's decision to ignore Islamabad.

Several months after the new order, in August and September 2008, U.S. forces entered Pakistan's tribal areas on two occasions in order to raid suspected Taliban and al Qaeda sanctuaries. On September 3 two dozen members of the Navy Seals dismounted from two helicopters at Angoradda, a village in South Waziristan, and raided three houses late at night in search of the militants. The forces spent several hours on the ground and killed about twenty people, who they suspected of being al Qaeda operatives, though the validity of that claim was called into doubt when it was later revealed that most of the victims were women and children and belonged to one family.[6] The intrusion provoked an intense reaction from the Pakistani military, which fired at the helicopters and warned of retaliation if any more such operations were carried out. In a strongly worded statement General Kayani warned that Pakistan would not allow foreign troops on its soil and that the country's sovereignty and integrity would be defended at all cost. Then, on September 19, Kayani flew to meet Adm. Mike Mullen, chairman of the U.S. Joint Chiefs of Staff, on the aircraft carrier USS *Abraham Lincoln* and gave him the toughest possible warning against any future intrusion.

Yet by some reports, in his first meeting with the Bush administration later in September, President Zardari gave his consent to unrestricted drone strikes even without prior approval of Pakistani authorities, which was an abrupt departure from Islamabad's past policy of allowing only limited action with the military's consent.[7] Zardari was clearly eager to show his support for the United States, but his cooperation provoked widespread public anger. The public generally perceived such operations, as well as the ongoing drone strikes, as blatant violations of Pakistani sovereignty.

What could not be denied about the drone strikes was that they had produced some significant breakthroughs in the killing of top al Qaeda leadership. On January 29, 2008, a Predator strike had killed Abu Laith al-Libbi, a top-tier al Qaeda leader who was believed to have been involved in an attempt to assassinate Vice President Dick Cheney when he was on a visit to Bagram Air Force Base in Afghanistan in February 2007.[8] He was said to be a key link between al Qaeda and its affiliates in North Africa, and his killing was the most serious blow to the group's top leadership in several years.

Seventeen more known drone attacks in 2008 reportedly killed at least eight other senior al Qaeda operatives, including Abu Sulayman Al-Jazair, Midhat Mursi, Khalid Habib, Abu Akash, Mohammad Hasan Khalil al-Hakim (alias Abu Jihad al-Masri), Abdullah Azam al-Saudi, British al Qaeda operative Rashid Rauf, and Abu Zubair al-Masri. The deaths of Midhat Mursi, a bomb maker and chemical weapons expert, and Khalid Habib, the group's operations chief in Pakistan and Afghanistan, were particularly damaging blows.[9] Fifty more drone attacks in 2009 eliminated several other senior al Qaeda and militant commanders.[10]

A missile strike in South Waziristan on New Year's day killed Usama al-Kini, head of al Qaeda's operations in Pakistan, and his lieutenant, Sheikh Ahmed Salim Swedan. Both were on the FBI's Most Wanted list and had been indicted for the 1998 bombings of U.S. embassies in Tanzania and Kenya, the countries in which they were born.[11] They were also believed to have trained operatives to travel to the United States and Europe. Usama al-Kini was blamed for several terrorist attacks in Pakistan, including the bombing of Islamabad's Marriott Hotel in September 2008, which left fifty-five people dead, including several U.S. security officials. He was also suspected of involvement in the plot to kill Benazir Bhutto when she returned to Pakistan on October 18, 2007.

Tahir Yuldashev, the chief of the Islamic Movement of Uzbekistan, fell victim to a Predator strike on Kanigoram, a town in South Waziristan, on August 27, 2009. The Uzbek commander had been closely associated with al Qaeda and the Pakistani Taliban movement and had led the resistance against the Pakistani military.

From 2007 to 2009 at least twelve of the top twenty high-value al Qaeda operatives, along with dozens of lesser figures, are believed to have been killed by drones, and many bases and safe houses were also destroyed.[12] The success of the drone strikes, however, came at high human and political costs. According to one estimate, more than seventy strikes between 2006 and 2009 killed more than seven hundred civilians and only fourteen al Qaeda leaders, and in July 2009 the Brookings Institution in Washington released a report stating that ten civilians died in the drone attacks for every militant killed.[13]

The secret campaign provoked condemnation from many international rights groups. On June 3, 2009, the United Nations Human Rights Council (UNHRC) delivered a report sharply critical of U.S. tactics and asserting that the U.S. government had failed to keep track of the civilian casualties or to provide means for citizens of affected nations to obtain information about the casualties and any legal inquests regarding them. Washington responded by claiming that any such information held by the U.S. military was kept inaccessible to the public due to the high level of secrecy surrounding the drone attack program.[14]

On October 27, 2009, a UNHRC investigator, Philip Alston, called on the United States to demonstrate that it was not randomly killing people in violation of international law through its use of drones on the Afghan border. Alston criticized Washington's refusal to respond to the UN's concerns until then and said, "Otherwise you have the really problematic bottom line, which is that the Central Intelligence Agency is running a program that is killing significant numbers of people and there is absolutely no accountability in terms of the relevant international laws."[15]

More worrying, the drone campaign had also contributed to a great swelling of anti-American sentiment in Pakistan. A poll by Gallup Pakistan in 2009 found only 9 percent of Pakistanis in favor of the attacks and 67 percent against, with a majority ranking the United States as a greater threat to Pakistan than its archrival, India, or the Pakistani Taliban.[16] The growing public resentment led many Pakistani political figures to publicly condemn the operations. "Continued drone attacks in FATA have proved counterproductive and have seriously impeded Pakistan's efforts towards rooting out militancy and terrorism from that area," Prime Minister Yusuf Raza Gilani told Ambassador Richard Holbrooke on July 21, 2009.[17]

Such pronouncements became a ritual for Pakistani leaders when U.S. officials visited, but they were only for public consumption. Off the record generals and politicians alike generally voiced support for the strikes, and the government secretly continued to supply crucial intelligence to the CIA, helping to identify targets.[18] Some Pakistani security officials and analysts also dismissed the estimates of civilian casualties as greatly exaggerated, contending that the number of civilians killed was actually very low and that most of those deaths occurred because militants had been hiding in the houses of local residents.

The double-talk further eroded the already highly questionable credibility of the Pakistani government and reinforced the public perception of its inability to prevent foreign intrusion and defend the country's sovereignty, as well as causing a great deal of resentment in the military among middle- and low-ranking officials, raising fears of division within the ranks. The drone strikes also fed a growing perception of the United States as a cowardly enemy, unwilling to shed its own blood in battle. A particularly pernicious effect was to drive more recruits to the militant groups, as, according to tribal code, the families of drone victims were required to seek revenge.

Perhaps the most compelling criticism of the secret campaign, however, was the assertion that it could not win the war. The killing of senior al Qaeda operatives and Taliban leaders produced only short-term gains, the argument went, as those leaders were quickly replaced by new, younger, and more radical men.[19] The strikes had also done nothing to stop the spread of the Pakistani Taliban and the wave of suicide bombings that were terrorizing the country. That was in part because the CIA had targeted so few Pakistani militants, instead continuing to concentrate on al Qaeda operatives despite the urging of Pakistani officials to pursue their homegrown insurgents.

This was one reason the killing of Baitullah Mehsud by a drone attack in August 2009 was considered so significant, even meeting the approval of the local residents, who had suffered so much under Baitullah's hand. As one local official asserted, "The tribesmen will support even a devil to rid them of the Taliban and al Qaeda."[20] And yet, as the military was to learn shortly thereafter, Baitullah's forces regrouped quickly after his killing and were to present the military with one of its toughest fights in the entire campaign to oust the militants. The battle on the ground against the increasingly powerful Pakistani Taliban demonstrated just how tenacious the militant forces were and how readily they could restore their control over territory they had been pushed out of. A glaring example was the Swat Valley, which the military had fought so vigorously to clear of Fazlullah's forces in 2007, but which had steadily fallen back under his control since then.

The militants had simply temporarily retreated into the surrounding mountains and shortly began a new advance on the valley. About three thousand militants pushed four times as many soldiers out of the valley in eighteen months of fighting from August 2007 to February 2009, leaving some fifteen hundred people dead.[21] In yet another humiliating concession, the government signed a peace agreement that February with Fazlullah, brokered on his behalf by his seventy-eight-year-old father-in-law, Sufi Mohammed, allowing him to establish Islamic Sharia rule there. The government had conceded to all of the Taliban's demands, including the establishment of Islamic courts, to be headed by clerics.

Pakistani officials touted the deal as a way to restore order in the bloodied region—just a few hours' drive from the capital—and to halt the Taliban's advance, but the truth that a highly demoralized army had no appetite to continue the fight there was totally apparent. The newly elected Zardari government as well as public opinion also favored an end to violence, even at the cost of accepting Taliban rule in the valley. The nation was in complete denial of the larger threat that appeasement posed to Pakistan's national security.

Government officials defended the deal by arguing that it reflected the will of the people. "It is in no way a sign of the state's weakness. The public will of the population of the Swat region is at the centre of all efforts and it should be taken into account while debating the merits of this agreement," said Sherry Rehman, the information minister of the Zardari government.[22] The accord, which had been pushed especially hard by the military, was even described as an arrangement that could be emulated in other areas. Buying peace was perceived to be the need of the hour, and it was true that many of the locals, who had suffered so much during the past two years of violence, supported the peace accord in the hope that it might bring an end to their misery. Many of them found the Taliban's promises of speedy justice and equality attractive.

This appeasement was to have huge costs in the weeks to come. It was quite evident from the outset that the Taliban were not going to be content with control over the Swat, and they used the deal not only to strengthen their hold in the valley but also to expand their influence. Shortly thereafter thousands more militants poured into the valley and set up training camps, quickly reestablishing it as one of the main bases for Taliban fighters. By March 2009 the number of militant fighters in the valley was believed to be between six thousand and eight thousand, nearly double the number at the end of 2008.[23]

Taliban leaders made no secret of their ultimate aim. "Our objective is to drive out Americans and their lackeys from Pakistan and Afghanistan," Muslim Khan, a spokesman for the group, told me in April when I interviewed him in his headquarters in the village of Imamdehri. The white-bearded militant leader had helped spearhead the group's two-year uprising in the valley. In his fifties now, Muslim Khan had spent many years in the late 1990s in the United States, where he lived in Boston and painted houses for a living. He had worked in the early 1980s as a student activist for the Pakistan People's Party, and later briefly joined one of the country's Islamist religious parties. By the time he reached Boston his anti-Western views had hardened, and he had been associated with the Islamic militant movement since his return to Pakistan in 2002. With his choppy English he had become the Taliban's main contact with foreign journalists.

He showed me a list of people whom the Taliban planned to try in the Islamic courts in the Swat, which included senior government officials and a woman whose husband is in the U.S. military. "These kinds of people should not live," he said with a smug smile on his face. He appeared particularly per-turbed about the presence of white Western women among the NATO forces in Afghanistan. "As long as these infidels are present in our land, it is our duty to fight them," he said.

The Taliban immediately took control of the local govern-ment offices, and the police were ordered to shed their uni-forms in favor of the traditional *shalwar kameez*, an outfit comprising a long shirt and loose trousers. Women were no longer allowed to leave their home without their husband or a male blood relative. Girls schools were reopened after initially being closed, but the students had to be covered from head to toe, and Taliban officials routinely inspected classrooms for violators. Floggings and executions quickly commenced.

I was shocked when, on April 12, 2009, I went to a gather-ing hosted by top regional government officials at the official residence of Syed Mohammed Javed, the commissioner of the Malakand division, of which the Swat Valley is a part. The affair was apparently a celebration of the Taliban takeover of the region, and I saw several senior Taliban commanders in attendance. Sitting in a corner of a large veranda crammed with gun-wielding Taliban fighters I saw them arriving one by one with their armed escorts. There was Muslim Khan, with his unruly long hair cascading down from his black turban, walking arrogantly past the police and paramilitary soldiers. Senior government officials lined up to receive the man who was responsible for ordering the execution of innocent children and women, who just hours before had shown me the list of future targets.

More shock was in store when later that evening I saw Faqir Mohammed, one of the top leaders of Tehrik-e-Taliban Pakistan who had spearheaded the ongoing bloody war against Pakistani forces in the neighboring Bajaur tribal region, walking in with a large entourage. Escorted by an Uzbek bodyguard, he was whisked inside a large hall, where the other Taliban commanders squatted on a carpeted floor. The Pakistani government placed a $200,000 bounty on his head in 2009. The presence of one of the most wanted militant leaders at the official residence of a top regional bureaucrat when thousands of army soldiers were engaged in bloody war against his men in Bajaur was astonishing.

As should have been expected, after consolidating their hold on the Swat the emboldened militants began to push into neighboring areas. Within days of the peace accord they swept through the Dir district, which borders the Bajaur tribal region. Their next destination was the Shangla district, located close to the strategic Karakoram Highway, connecting northern Pakistan with China. And in the first week of April 2009 they overpowered a village militia in the adjacent Buner district, just seventy miles from Islamabad. Buner, with a population of more than 1.5 million and famous for its fruit orchards and granite, had traditionally opposed the Taliban, repulsing many attacks. It was considered a stronghold of the Awami National Party, a secular Pashtun nationalist group, which headed the coalition government in the North West Frontier Province. The locals were prepared to resist the Taliban this time too, but the local administration ordered them not to fight. As the heavily armed militants streamed in, terrified residents fled their homes en masse, and within days the militants had seized control of the entire district. Hooded fighters carrying rocket launchers and machine-guns ransacked the offices of international aid and development agencies working in the district and took away their vehicles, and some employees of the agencies were briefly taken hostage. The Taliban set up Sharia courts in all of the newly controlled districts, and from the mosques they called local youth to join them. The people had little choice but to surrender.

The advance of the militants so close to Islamabad was a devastating blow to the government's claim that the peace deal would contain the Taliban. The accord had clearly been an abject failure, and the United States and other members of the international community urged the Pakistani government to reverse course. Describing the Taliban as an "existentialist threat," U.S. Secretary of State Hillary Clinton urged Pakistanis worldwide to oppose the government's policy of yielding to them. Pakistanis "need to speak out forcefully against a policy that is ceding more and more territory to the insurgents," Clinton testified before a House committee.[24] But even in the face of a storm of criticism, the government and the military continued to defend the deal for some time, arguing that it might yet work and that it was their only viable option. They also compared the deal to local alliances forged by the United States in Afghanistan and Iraq.

In Washington more attention was now focused on Pakistan than on the war in Afghanistan. The Taliban advance raised huge concerns just as President Barack Obama was about to unveil his new Af-Pak strategy. Announced on March

27, 2009, the strategy bolstered U.S. forces in Afghanistan and set a benchmark for progress in fighting al Qaeda and the Taliban there and in Pakistan. "The era of the blank check is over," Obama declared. The message was clear that U.S. aid would now be linked to Pakistan's efforts to counter militancy.

But many worried that the militants' insurgency had raged out of control. Militants loyal to Baitullah Mehsud had stepped up their attacks on Pakistani security forces in South Waziristan and in the Orakzai and Khyber tribal regions. In March the three most powerful Taliban commanders—Baitullah Mehsud, Hafiz Gul Bahadur, and Malwi Nazir, based in North and South Waziristan—had set aside their differences to form a United Mujahideen Council. It was apparent that the militants were gearing up to escalate their activities on both sides of the border. The Swat debacle raised the nightmare possibility of an escalating, widening, simultaneous two-country war. For the United States, Britain, and their allies, the looming specter was not one failed state, but two.

The deadlock over the deal finally began to give way when a Pakistani television station broadcast a Taliban flogging of a seventeen-year-old girl in a Swat village for coming out of her house unaccompanied by a blood relative. Public opinion turned dramatically against the militants, which increased the pressure on the military to act. Then Sufi Mohammed rejected the judges appointed by the government to preside over the Sharia courts in the Swat, claiming that they didn't fulfill the requirements of Islam. He further declared that the government didn't have the authority to appoint the judges, calling democracy un-Islamic and saying there was no need for a constitution in the country when it has the Quran. "All those who believe in democracy are infidels," he said in an interview with a private Pakistani television station.[25]

Then, in the last week of April, the militants kidnapped four officers of the Pakistani Special Forces from a market in Mingora, the main town of the Swat, and paraded them before the media. Days later their decapitated bodies were found; it was to be the last straw. As the military prepared to launch a new offensive, political support for the move built.

While the mainstream political parties had earlier favored soft-peddling with the Taliban, they now changed their views, and the Obama administration played an important role in getting the parties onboard. The support of Nawaz Sharif was deemed especially important, given his long ties to Islamist political parties; if he would come out for strong action, that would be particularly persuasive with the Pakistani public. Richard Holbrooke, the U.S. special envoy to Pakistan and Afghanistan, was in constant contact with him. Holbrooke's intensity had sometimes alienated Pakistanis, but he had developed excellent relations with Zardari as well as with Sharif. "I very much like him. He constantly keeps in touch with me," the former prime minister told me.[26]

As expected, Sharif's decision to support a new military offensive in the Swat Valley helped sway the rest of the key parties, as well as the public. In the first week of May the army launched a three-pronged offensive involving approximately thirty thousand troops, backed by air force jets and helicopter gunships, turning a large area of the Swat Valley into a battle zone. Most of these troops were moved from the eastern border after the United States assured Pakistan that India would not make a move after the troops left. Thousands of counterinsurgency commandos were dropped by helicopter into a mountainous Taliban stronghold in the Piochar region. They had been trained under a new program for fighting in the region's tough mountainous terrain funded by the United States and had proven highly effective in recent assaults in the Bajaur tribal region. It was the bloodiest battle yet in what has been called a war for the survival of Pakistan.

There were an estimated five thousand Taliban militants in the mountainous terrain, 10,000 feet (3,050 meters) above sea level, which was regarded as the main militant command-and-control center. Some top insurgent leaders, including Mullah Fazlullah, were believed to have been hiding there. "Our main strategy is to block the free movement of the militants and eliminate the entire leadership," declared Maj. Gen. Athar Abbas, the main military spokesman.

A fierce battle ensued, in which Pakistani forces used heavy artillery and helicopter gunships, forcing the residents to flee their homes. Almost one million people from Swat, Buner, and Dir took refuge in neighboring districts. But hundreds of thousands of others were trapped, and the militants who had taken positions in some residential areas used them as shields. The insurgents had also mined the main roads, making it extremely difficult for the people to flee.

The exodus was an unprecedented humanitarian crisis that threatened to undermine public support for the military campaign. Refugees arrived—bedraggled, exhausted, and crammed into buses, vans, and trucks—at a host of makeshift camps outside Swat. They had left to escape the army's shelling and the Taliban attacks, but displaced from their homes they faced hunger, exposure, and uncertainty about their future as the government struggled to cope with the worst catastrophe in its sixty-two years. International humanitarian aid was slow to come. The government's inability to cope with the flood of refugees provoked intense public outrage, opening a window for Islamist political parties. Jamaat-e-Islami, which had openly opposed the army operation against the militants, was very active in all the camps, providing the refugees with all kinds of help. Members of banned radical groups were also seen working there.

The damage to homes and businesses in the region was devastating. When I visited in the second week of May the deserted road through the town of Ambela, with a population of about ten thousand, was littered with burned vehicles, spent artillery rounds, and broken electricity pylons. Many of the houses were damaged by shelling and riddled with bullet holes. On the corner of the main street Amir Basha examined his smashed grocery shop and contemplated the mounting cost of the Pakistani Army's assault on the Taliban. He and his family had fled the fighting, taking refuge in the northwestern city of Peshawar, but came back three weeks later to inspect the damage during a brief lull in a curfew imposed by the army. "I don't think my family can return home soon," he muttered, shaking his head in despair.

In the third week of May troops stormed up jagged, rubble-strewn slopes to the village of Biny Baba Ziarat, on the 7,500-foot-high mountain ridge overlooking the picturesque Swat Valley. The fighting had raged for two weeks as the Pakistani military struggled to dislodge the militants from their highest stronghold. The village's capture was heralded as a sign of the success of the month-old offensive. A green and white Pakistani flag fluttered over the windy encampment, and army troops dug in on a strategic ridge that until two days earlier had been held by the Taliban. A labyrinth of caves and underground bunkers equipped with electricity and air vents had served as the insurgents' main military and communication base. The facility pointed to a disciplined and well-funded adversary with a fighting force believed to be in the thousands. The vast complex with panoramic views of the valley on all sides had been built by the Taliban in the past, when they virtually controlled the region.

The heights were first bombed by jets and helicopters, leaving several large craters, before troops stormed it and took control. "They fought till the last men," said Lt. Col. Mohammed Riaz, who led the final charge. Pointing toward one cave that had been destroyed by shelling, he said, "Some one hundred bodies are probably still buried inside one of them." The cave mouths and bunkers were made with brick walls several feet thick and topped with large tree trunks, dirt, and leaves. Flies buzzed in and out of a cave well stocked with food. Outside stood a bullet-scarred wheelbarrow filled with lentils.

Biny Baba Ziarat was not just the Taliban's military base; it was also used as a training center for young men they had forcibly recruited. Textbooks belonging to students who underwent guerrilla training were scattered inside a cave. Mohammed Akhtar, a fourteen-year-old schoolboy who was apprehended on the site, had been brought there about five months earlier to be trained as a suicide bomber. "There were dozens of young boys in the camp," he said, looking terrified after being rescued by security forces.

After the takeover of Biny Baba Ziarat, the commanding officer, Gen. Sajjad Ghani, said, "We cannot give any timeline for the end of fighting. The hardcore militants will never surrender. We have to eliminate them." [27] Echoing those sentiments, Col. Abdul Rehman told me, "Fighting an insurgency in your own country is hell." But the morale of the troops seemed high, in large part due to the widespread public support. "When the whole country is behind you, you feel better," Rehman said.

After gaining control of the northern Swat districts of Khawazkhela and Matta, troops pushed toward Mingora, the main city in the valley, approached from three sides. Most of the city's 200,000 people had already fled, but a sizable population and a group of government officials remained trapped, with dwindling food, water, and fuel. Decomposed bodies lay unattended in many parts of the city; the people were too afraid to collect them.

The battle for Mingora, a city of narrow alleys and congested residential quarters, presented a decisive test of the military's ability to defeat the Taliban in Swat. The militants had occupied the rooftops and the main buildings and were well entrenched for a pitched battle. After bloody street-to-street fighting, the troops cleared Mingora on May 31, 2009, but though a large number of militants had been killed, many others, including their top leaders, had escaped.

In July 2009 the government declared the Swat Valley secured, and ignoring a warning issued by international relief organizations that the security situation was still dangerous, residents streamed back home. Families with young children waited for hours in the sweltering heat to be allowed to enter the war zone. "It is a long wait but I am happy to go back home," said Wali Rehman, a grocer, who was traveling with twenty members of his extended family crammed into a van with a white flag fluttering on top.

For many it was not a joyous homecoming. Their crops and homes had been destroyed, and shops and businesses were closed. "I hope there will be no fighting here any more," Abdul Wadood, a shop owner in Mingora, said to me as he dusted off clothes racks. Police and civilian administration personnel had started returning to their posts, and the electricity supply had been restored, but it would take a long time for people like Wadood to revive their businesses and resume normal life.

Many also feared that the Taliban would return yet again. "The army promised us twice before that they cleared the area, but then the Taliban came again and again. Perhaps this time the Taliban will come again," Bakht Rawan, a local trader, told me. The escape of the top militant leadership, including Fazlullah, was a major cause for concern that those who feared the Taliban's return might be right. The military, how-ever, dismissed such fears, declaring that there was no possi-bility of the Taliban's regrouping. "Their capacity to regroup and launch major attacks has been destroyed," said a senior official.[28] The army was going to stay in the area to ensure its safety. But they did not rule out the possibility of a long-drawn-out guerrilla war.

The military may have succeeded in seizing control of the valley, but the region continued to bleed. Civilians who had suffered at the hands of the Taliban went on revenge kill-ings. The people of Swat had long been used to the sight of bullet-riddled bodies dumped on the streets; the bodies used to be those of government officials, policemen, or women killed by the Taliban. That pattern of death was reversed after the region fell to the military. The Taliban were hunted down by the security forces and families of the victims of their atrocities. The bodies of militants were regularly found hang-ing from electricity poles and bridges in towns and villages. In many cases notes were left on the bodies warning that such would be the fate of all enemies of the state and Swat. Some of the notes urged people not to remove the bodies, borrow-ing from Taliban dictates at the height of their power. Some officials justified the killings, arguing, "When people see the bodies of the top commanders, it helps to remove their fear," as a senior army officer asserted.[29]

The military success in Swat dealt a serious blow to the Taliban, and it won the praise of the United States and other Western allies, but it also prompted the Taliban to expand the guerrilla war into the country's heartland. There was a marked increase in suicide attacks on the security forces and installations around the country in the months that followed. The fight against the insurgents was far from over.

CHAPTER 7

Breaking Apart
the Myth

The men in crisp military fatigues riding in a white Suzuki van with a military registration plate evoked no suspicion. The guards at the first security checkpoint waved them right through. It was around ten in the morning on October 10, 2009, and thousands of army officers and staff were already settled in at their workstations inside the sprawling compound known as Army General Headquarters, or simply GHQ. Security at the complex, which was right in the heart of a bustling commercial district of Rawalpindi, had been beefed up after the surge in attacks targeting military personnel and installations. The several security checkpoints had been strengthened and the access roads were closed to civilian traffic.

As the van made its way past the checkpoint, gunmen suddenly jumped out and started firing indiscriminately. Several explosions shook the ground, and under cover of the firing and the thick smoke the gunmen ran toward the heavy iron gates. Apparently out of nowhere appeared another group of gunmen in uniform, and before the guards could realize what was happening several of them were shot. An intense firefight broke out when the soldiers in the watchtowers began firing on the intruders, killing three of them and injuring another. Gunmen coming up just behind the injured attacker then shot their wounded colleague dead in an attempt to confuse the guards. The trick worked: the guards made no attempt to stop the attackers as they rushed through the open gate of the complex toward a one-storey building that housed the offices of Pakistan's military intelligence.

Brig. Anwar ul-Haq, the director of security, was in a conference in his office in the building when the melee broke out. Interrupting the meeting and rushing into the hallway, he saw a man in military uniform with his back turned to him and called out, "Move away from there." The man turned around and shot him dead. Another bullet killed Lt. Col. Waseem Amir, who had rushed out to the hall behind the brigadier. GHQ protocol prohibits carrying a gun inside the complex, and as a result the assailants faced no resistance from the officers: everyone was unarmed.

The assailants took thirty-nine officers and civilians hostage and divided them into two groups. Twenty-two were herded into one room by three assailants, one of whom wore a suicide jacket. He sat on a table in the middle of the room while the others hung a banner behind him inscribed with verses from the Quran. The remaining seventeen hostages were guarded in a second room by an assailant also wearing a suicide jacket. The intruders then filled both rooms with explosives.

The gunmen verbally abused the hostages and accused the Pakistani military of fighting America's war and killing its own people. They spoke partly in English, indicating that they were well educated.

Gen. Ashfaq Kayani, Pakistan's army chief, was in his office at the time of the attack, less than a hundred meters from the building under siege. The assailants were just a gunshot away from the country's top commander. That morning the general was scheduled for a meeting with the president and the prime minister in Islamabad. When the assault occurred he was driven out of the complex by the back gate, returning a few hours later to monitor the situation.

The assailants presented a list of demands, including that some one hundred Pakistani and Afghan Taliban commanders being held by the security forces be freed. Among those on the list was a woman named Aafia Siddiqui, who faced trial in a New York court on a charge of assault with a deadly weapon and attempting to kill U.S. soldiers in Afghanistan.[1] An MIT-trained Pakistani neuroscientist, Siddiqui was accused by the United Nations and the United States of being an al Qaeda member and named one of the seven Most Wanted al Qaeda figures by the FBI. She had disappeared from Karachi in March 2003 after the arrest of Khalid Sheikh Mohammed, the alleged mastermind of the 9/11 terrorist attacks, with whom she had close ties. After divorcing her first husband in 2003, she had married a nephew of Khalid Sheikh Mohammed, who was later arrested and sent to the U.S. government's Guantánamo Bay detention camp.[2] Siddiqui's family claimed that she and her three children had been illegally detained and interrogated at that time by Pakistani intelligence, likely at the behest of the United States.

Siddiqui was arrested outside the compound of the governor of Ghazni province in Afghanistan on July 17, 2008, and was badly wounded in a shooting incident at a U.S. military detention center following her arrest. She was flown to the United States, where she was charged with two counts of attempted murder and armed assault on U.S. officers and employees, and her arrest and trial had become a rallying point for Islamists in Pakistan.

The attackers were clearly not calling the shots in the operation, as they were constantly on their cell phones getting instructions. As negotiations dragged on, in the cover of darkness Pakistani Special Forces surrounded the building. At five in the morning, about nineteen hours after the attack, with the hostage takers clearly growing weary, commandos stormed the rooms where the hostages were held. They successfully killed the would-be bomber in the room with the twenty-two hostages before he could detonate his suicide jacket, but two commandos were killed by return fire. As other commandos approached the second room, the second suicide bomber blew himself up, bringing down the roof. The explosives in the room were also detonated, killing two hostages. In total, nineteen people, including nine soldiers and eight attackers, were killed in the bloody standoff. All of the other captives were rescued, and the soldiers managed to capture one of the assailants, though the rest of them were killed.

The Pakistani Army's prestige was badly tarnished by the assault. This was neither the first attack on an army installation in the country nor the most deadly, but it was undoubtedly the most serious. The attackers had pulled off a security breach at one of the most sensitive national defense establishments in the country and had threatened the safety of the army chief and his top commanders. They clearly also had intimate knowledge of the layout of the complex, indicating that military personnel had been involved.

The success of the attack was all the more shocking because the Criminal Investigation Department, a unit of the police force, had warned that militants were planning an assault on the headquarters. In a letter to the intelligence agencies, the CID had predicted that the militants would dress in military uniforms and try to take hostages, and specifically stated that militants belonging to the Pakistani Taliban would join forces with other militant groups in the attack. The informa-

tion was reportedly based in part on interrogations of suspects involved in the attack on the Sri Lankan cricket team in
Lahore in March 2009.[3] Amazingly the contents of the letter
were published a week before the attack in a leading national
newspaper, and still the army had not been prepared. Some
argued that the army's failure was due to poor coordination
and to distrust between the civilian agencies and the military.
A number of officials argued, unconvincingly, that it was difficult to prevent such an attack even if it was expected.

One thing about the attack was perfectly clear: the militants
were sending the message that despite the setback in the Swat
Valley, they still had the capacity to hit even the most secure
government installations. They were also aiming to demor-
alize the military and weaken public support for the coming
South Waziristan offensive, the preparations for which were
getting to their final stages. Azam Tariq, a Taliban spokesman,
claimed the assault was to avenge Baitullah Mehsud's death.
"This was our first small effort and a present to the Pakistani
and American governments," he said, adding that the raid had
been carried out by a Punjabi faction. He warned of similar
operations in other parts of the country.[4]

Investigations later revealed that the attack was a joint operation by the Taliban and elements of a number of outlawed
Pakistani militant groups, such as Jaish-e-Mohammed and
Lashkar-e-Jhangvi, which are dominated by militants from
Punjab.[5] Five of the ten attackers came from Waziristan; the
other five were from Punjab and the North West Frontier
Province. Such collaboration had been revealed behind a number of other recent terrorist attacks in major Pakistani cities,
signaling the deeply troubling establishment of strong bases
of support for militant terrorism in the heartland and the evo-
lution of an ever more intertwined nexus between highly educated professionals, former and current military personnel,

and the leadership in the Taliban and al Qaeda in the tribal regions. The growing network in the Punjab had organized a number of suicide bombings and daring daylight gun battles in the provincial capital of Lahore as well as the twin cities of Rawalpindi and Islamabad. Many of these attacks were masterminded by al Qaeda but executed by its allies among the new breed of local militants.[6]

One of the most shocking such attacks was that on the Marriott Hotel in the heart of Islamabad in September 2008. The Marriott, the city's top hotel, was located right in the heart of the capital's high-security zone, less than one kilometer from the presidential palace and Parliament House. The massive suicide car bombing killed more than fifty people, including several foreign nationals, and was one of the worst terrorist attacks in Pakistan's history. The apparent targets were U.S. military personnel who were reportedly staying there.[7]

A twenty-seven-year-old chemical engineer named Syed Abraruddin was among those who planned the attack. Coming from a prosperous middle-class family in the northwestern city of Mardan, Abraruddin grew up in Saudi Arabia, where his father was working, before returning to Pakistan to complete his higher education. He graduated from Edwards College in Peshawar, one of the top academic institutions in northwestern Pakistan, set up by the British colonial administration almost a century earlier, and he later joined the faculty of an engineering university. He had come into contact with Islami Jamiat Talba, the student wing of the Jamaat-e-Islami Party at that university, and later joined al Badar, a militant outfit linked with the JI, which brought him into contact with al Qaeda. He eventually made his way to Waziristan and rose to a key position in the militant leadership. "He is a brilliant planner and is very close to the al Qaeda leaders," said a senior investigator who had closely monitored his activities.[8]

Abraruddin had recruited many other educated young men to his group. One was Mohammed Imran, who had assisted in the planning of the Marriott bombing. Imran was also well educated, having earned a university degree in business administration, and he came from a well-educated family. His father was in the construction business, and Imran himself had worked with an international nongovernmental organization. He had gotten involved with militant activities through a body-building club in Peshawar, and he had also gone for training in Waziristan.

An event that underscored the role of disaffected military personnel in the increasing sophistication of the militant attacks was the assassination of retired Maj. Gen. Ameer Faisal Alvi on a crisp November morning in 2008 near his home on the outskirts of Islamabad. A husky man in his mid-fifties, General Alvi had a reputation as a brilliant but hot-headed officer. He had been promoted to major general in 2003 and became the first general commanding officer of the elite Special Services Group, which was responsible for fighting the militants. As the head of the commando force, General Alvi was credited with spearheading some of the most daring actions against al Qaeda in the lawless tribal regions.

In one such action, in October 2003, his troops raided a militant hideout in a border town in South Waziristan, killing some al Qaeda members and capturing a number of others, who were later handed over to the Americans. Among those killed in the assault was Ahmad Said Abdur Rehman Khadr al Kanadi, a Canadian national of Egyptian origin.[9] A close lieutenant of Osama bin Laden, Khadr was designated a high-ranking al Qaeda member by the United Nations. The operation boosted General Alvi's profile in the army, but it also made him a prime al Qaeda target.

On that morning, as his car was stalled in expressway traf-

fic, three gunmen jumped out of a car that had been trailing
him and unleashed a hail of bullets on the general's vehicle,
killing him instantly. The precision of the attack and the fact
that the gunmen had used 9 mm pistols, standard army issue,
led to speculation that army personnel were involved. An
investigation later determined that the murder was ordered
by al Qaeda to avenge the killing of Khadr and other militants
by General Alvi's Special Forces, and that one of the assassins
was Haroon Ashiq, a retired army major who the investigators
determined had been working with al Qaeda-affiliated militants based in the Waziristan tribal region.[10]

Haroon was representative of a cadre of young officers
who had left the forces to join the militant cause. Coming
from Pakistani-controlled Kashmir, he had reportedly been
incensed by the Pakistani government's decision to support
the U.S. invasion of Afghanistan. His younger brother, Captain
Khuram, who had served with General Alvi's Special Services
force, had also quit the army, joining the Taliban in fighting
the U.S.-led coalition forces in Afghanistan. He was killed on
the battlefield in 2007, in Helmand province, further stoking
his brother's zealotry.

Major Haroon's journey to jihad began when he joined
Lashkar-e-Taiba, the country's most powerful militant group
fighting the Indian forces in Kashmir. His association with the
group was short-lived, however, because he became disenchanted with the group for limiting its operations to Kashmir. He next joined a group of militants organized by Ilyas
Kashmiri, whom Haroon had known for some time and who
was affiliated with al Qaeda. Ilyas Kashmiri had been arrested
as part of the investigation into a failed attempt to assassinate President Musharraf in December 2003, but was set free
for lack of evidence. He then fled to Waziristan, where he
organized the 313 Brigade, comprising elements of various

outlawed militant groups, to fight against the Pakistani government and operating in affiliation with al Qaeda.

It was through Ilyas Kashmiri that Major Haroon was introduced to al Qaeda operatives, and the assassination of General Alvi was the first major assignment given to him by al Qaeda. The major, who assumed the nom de guerre Abu Khatab, also provided training to the militants in Waziristan, and he was later given the task of raising funds through the kidnapping of wealthy businessmen for ransom. In 2008 he kidnapped Saatish Annand, a well-known filmmaker from Karachi, and took him to Waziristan, where he was kept in captivity for six months; he was released after his family agreed to pay millions of dollars in ransom. Haroon was arrested in April 2009 during an attempt to bring another kidnapped businessman to Waziristan. During interrogations that revealed these details, he is said to have expressed no remorse for his actions.[11]

At least some of the GHQ attackers were of this new breed, and some had been involved in prior notorious raids. Mohammed Aqeel, the sole surviving gunman who was captured from the scene of the GHQ attack, was believed to be the leader of the group. In his early thirties, Aqeel had served in the army's medical corps for more than six years before deserting in 2005. A resident of Kahuta, a northern Punjab district not far from Islamabad, Aqeel, who was a paramedic, was also known as Dr. Usman. He was associated with the Islamist groups Jaish-e-Mohammed and Lashkar-e-Jhangvi, and had moved to North Waziristan and joined an al Qaeda-affiliated group that staged attacks in Kashmir. His name surfaced on the list of Most Wanted terrorists when police named him in the attack on the Sri Lankan cricket team in March 2009. He was also the main suspect in the suicide bombing of Islamabad's Marriott Hotel in September 2008.[12]

As well as signaling that the insurgency had established deep roots in the heartland, the GHQ attack was a bold message that Baitullah Mehsud's death had by no means crippled his organization. The investigation into the attack revealed that the security services had intercepted a call before the attack from Waliur Rehman, a deputy to the slain Taliban leader, in which he asked his supporters, "Please pray for our mujahideen in their mission." [13]

Baitullah's killing had slowed attacks by Tehrik-e-Taliban Pakistan (TTP) for a time, as a struggle to replace him broke out between Rehman and another powerful figure in the movement, Hakimullah Mehsud. Rehman was badly wounded in a firefight between his supporters and those of Hakimullah in a Taliban council meeting held in August 2009 to choose Baitullah's successor; it was believed that Hakimullah had also been shot. Further armed confrontation was apparently averted after intervention by al Qaeda and some senior Afghan Taliban commanders, who were concerned that the infighting could split the TTP, not only in South Waziristan but also in other tribal regions. "You must follow the path of a great leader . . . and save your bullets for your true enemies," they were reminded. [14]

A deal was reached whereby Hakimullah became the TTP's overall chief, and Rehman remained in charge of the group's activities in South Waziristan, which gave him control of the Taliban's main fighting force from the Mehsud tribe, in recognition of his superior skills as a military commander. With the struggle resolved, the TTP, with the support of Punjabi militants, launched a series of spectacular terrorist strikes in addition to the GHQ attack, making it resoundingly clear that the group was back in full force.

· · ·

Several days before the army headquarters assault five people were killed when a bomber dressed in military fatigues walked through the security cordon at the World Food Program offices of the United Nations in Islamabad. On October 9 a suicide bomber blew up his explosives-laden vehicle in a congested marketplace in Peshawar, killing at least forty-nine people. Two days after the GHQ attack, on October 12, a suicide bomber struck in a crowded market in the northwestern town of Shangla, killing forty-one people, including several soldiers. This attack was all the more chilling because Shangla is in the Swat Valley, which had so recently been declared cleared of militants.

Then, on October 15, the TTP unleashed a devastating string of well-planned and audacious attacks on police and government installations across the country. During the course of the day assailants disguised as police and wielding guns and grenades attacked three security agency buildings in the country's second largest city, Lahore. A suicide car bomber targeted a police station in the northwestern city of Kohat, and a car bomb in the city of Peshawar was detonated remotely at a government residential complex.

The first attack came shortly after 9 a.m., when two gunmen burst into a building of the Federal Investigation Agency, a key arm of Pakistan's counterterrorism establishment in Lahore. After a brief firefight six people lay dead. Soon after, five gunmen in police uniforms scaled the walls of a police training center for Punjab's Elite Force. Police eventually gunned down the attackers, but four civilians were killed in the clash. A third team of four gunmen, also in police uniforms, scaled the walls of another police academy, which was a center for new recruits and had been assaulted in a similar style in March 2009. At least fourteen people were killed, including four of the attackers.

Such synchronized attacks, occurring just days after the raid on the army headquarters, badly shook the country, exposing major weaknesses in the nation's security apparatus and demonstrating that the TTP was capable of coordinating assaults in a short period over a wide geographic area. The escalation of violence also left no doubt that the TTP had developed the capacity to strike at will at the heart of Pakistan's security establishment. Many feared that the string of attacks proved that the TTP had gained the upper hand in the insurgency, but the Pakistani military argued otherwise. Military officials contended that they were instead a sign of the militants' desperation to forestall the South Waziristan operation.

For months the military had been pounding South Waziristan with air strikes and artillery, and thousands of people had fled the area in anticipation of a full-scale invasion. The gains achieved in the Swat Valley were vital, but not sufficient to rein in the insurgency. If South Waziristan remained under the control of the Taliban and al Qaeda, the fighting would surely continue to escalate, and many leaders of the Swat insurgency, including Mullah Fazlullah, were believed to have taken refuge in the area. The United States had also stressed that moving on South Waziristan was crucial in the effort to gain control over the larger Afghanistan-Pakistan border region and turn the tide in the war in Afghanistan. This time the military could not afford to walk away from the job halfway through. Dithering would only allow the Taliban to further expand their operations, and General Kayani had publicly vowed that he would not stop until the region was secured.

The long-awaited offensive began on October 17, 2009, with the deployment of more than forty-five thousand troops, backed by air force jets and helicopter gunships. The massive use of force was considered critical for winding up the operation before the arrival of the harsh winter, and with these troops added to those still deployed in the Swat, the size of the total force engaged in the fight reached 100,000, almost the same as the total number of NATO forces deployed across the border in Afghanistan.

South Waziristan was a much tougher challenge than the Swat in terms of terrain. Its remote mountains and treacherous ravines were perfect guerrilla territory. And unlike in the Swat, where the Taliban had alienated many of the locals, the soldiers sent to South Waziristan had to contend with a hostile population that had resisted outside rule for centuries. Key to the military's strategy were deals it had negotiated with two powerful tribal leaders in bordering North Waziristan. Malwi Nazir, who led his own faction of the Taliban, was opposed to Baitullah's policy of fighting Pakistani security forces and instigating suicide attacks on the Pakistani mainland, though his men were very active against NATO forces across the border in Afghanistan. The powerful Waziri militant commander Gul Bahadur had also agreed to secure a Pakistani military supply chain through his area.

Increased cooperation between the U.S. and Pakistani forces also played an important role, with drones providing high-quality intelligence about the locations and movements of the militant forces. The sharing of real-time video feeds, communication intercepts, and other information greatly facilitated the campaign and marked a substantial improvement in the relations between the Pakistani military and the Americans. A senior Pakistani military official confirmed that there had been a great deal of improvement in intelligence support to Pakistan in mid-2009. Video feeds from drones were relayed to a joint coordination center at a border crossing at the Khyber Pass, where a Pakistani military team monitored the video and sent it to command centers in Pakistan, a U.S. official said.[15]

The operation was also facilitated by the fact that South Waziristan has a much smaller population than the Swat, about 500,000 compared to two million, which allowed the army much more freedom to attack in force. Much of the population had fled their homes by the time the operation began, taking refuge in neighboring districts, and the commencement of fighting triggered an additional massive exodus of more than 250,000 tribesmen. Though the exodus aided the military operations, it presented an overwhelming challenge to the government, which had made insufficient preparations for health facilities, supplies of food and potable water, and shelter for the refugees. The ensuing discontent among the refugees led to outbreaks of violence, and some people accused the government of not even attempting to provide food and other basic necessities.

The military's resolve was firm nonetheless, and within the first week of the offensive, troops had seized control of the town of Kotkai, a militant stronghold and the hometown of the new Taliban chief, Hakimullah Mehsud. The fall of the town was a major blow to the militants, who had put up a fierce fight. "Every house in the area was a Taliban bunker and troops had to fight for every inch," said a senior commander.[16] Within another week the forces had dislodged the Taliban from most of their strongholds.

The next battle, in the town of Laddah, lasted several days and left the town utterly deserted, with most houses reduced to rubble by the intense army shelling. The nearby town of Sararogha, described as the Taliban's operational nerve center, was also reduced to a pile of mud bricks and twisted iron. In January 2008 militants had attacked a military base in the town and executed twenty-five soldiers, after which the post had been abandoned. The tables had now dramatically turned, and the fighting had been intense. The Taliban had built long tunnels in the mountains from which they were extremely difficult to dislodge. "We faced tough resistance. They are ferocious fighters," said Brig. Mohammed Shafiq, the officer in charge. He looked calm as gunshots rang out in the distance, where insurgents were still holding out.[17]

Amid the rubble sat a ramshackle student hostel, which the Taliban had used as their base. One of the rooms, whose roof had been blown off by a mortar shell, had served as a Sharia court, and a blood-stained shirt dangled on a fan. "No one should question the ruling of the Islamic court," read a Taliban high command directive hanging on the wall. Another part of the building had served as a school for suicide bombers, and booklets with detailed instructions for making bombs were scattered on the dusty floor, as well as ammunition and vests with pouches tailored for suicide bombers. This training center was thought to be a main source of the attackers who had unleashed havoc on the country in the prior weeks.[18]

Four weeks into the offensive the army marched on the town of Makin, the hometown of the late Taliban leader Baitullah Mehsud, which was also the Taliban's most fortified position in the region and served as TTP headquarters. After several days of fierce street-to-street battles, the military forces seized control of the town. The fall of this last fortress marked the establishment of the Pakistani Army's control of the region.

Among all the blood and destruction of the operation some key intelligence was discovered that confirmed the links between al Qaeda and the TTP. The faded German passport of an al Qaeda operative, Said Bahaji, who was part of the Hamburg terrorist cell involved in the September 11 attacks, was recovered inside a mud compound on a hilltop in the village of Shawangai, which was apparently used as an al Qaeda communication base. A close associate of one of the 9/11 hijackers, Mohammed Atta, the thirty-four-year-old Bahaji had been in Pakistan since early September 2001. The recovery of his passport provided the most definitive proof to date of the direct link between the Pakistani militants and al Qaeda's high command.[19]

The military had succeeded in clearing most of South Waziristan within eight weeks of the operation. "The myth has been broken that this was a graveyard for empires and that it would be a graveyard for the army," boasted an officer.[20] President Zardari described the success of the military operation in South Waziristan as proof of his government's resolve to fight militancy, and public support for the offensive swelled. There was also a good bit of skepticism expressed, though, about whether the militancy could be defeated by military means alone.

The toughened resolve of the Pakistani military had certainly resulted in huge gains, but the war was not over yet. Thousands of militants, including top leaders Fazlullah, Hakimullah, and Waliur Rehman, had escaped the offensive, fleeing to neighboring North Waziristan and the Orakzai tribal region, where they immediately began regrouping with the help of their allies among Pakistani militant groups there. Militant forces have, of course, regrouped and returned to once-cleared territory repeatedly in the past, and the Pakistani military would not be able to maintain a deployment of 100,000 troops in the regions indefinitely.

The attacks in urban centers also did not abate. In bold defiance of any claim to victory by the Pakistan Army, the TTP immediately unleashed a new string of bombings. On November 13 a devastating suicide car bomb attack was perpetrated on the regional office of the country's main intelligence agency, the ISI, in Lahore, leaving dozens of operatives dead and wounded. The city of Peshawar, a gateway to the tribal region, was hit particularly hard, with near daily bombings. Schools were closed down many days because of the fear of suicide bombings, and hundreds of civilians were killed in the attacks.

The level of violence was notched up to a new level when, on the cold afternoon of December 4, 2009, four gunmen stormed a packed mosque on Parade Lane, a five-minute drive from army headquarters, spraying gunfire and throwing hand grenades. Most of the two hundred worshippers gathered for Friday prayers were serving or retired army officers and their children. Two of the attackers blew themselves up, bringing down a part of the prayer hall, while the other two fired a storm of bullets into the crowd. As the worshippers ran for cover the gunmen singled out some for execution. "They took the people, got hold of their hair, and shot them," said a retired army officer who survived the attack. "Their objective was to kill and be killed." They particularly targeted children, shouting, "Now know how it feels when other people are killed in the bombings!"[21] Thirty-six people, including seventeen children, an army major general, and a brigadier general, were killed. The strain showed among Pakistani Army personnel as they buried their fellow officers and their children the next day. The attack was a devastating blow.

Again authorities believe that the attackers were of the new, highly educated breed. Most of those suspected to be involved in the planning and execution were affiliated with Jamaat-e-Islami, and one of those detained, who was later released, Raja Ehsan Aziz, a graduate of Columbia University, was a retired university professor. Aziz, whose wife, Amra Aziz, was a former member of the National Assembly from the party, had left the JI a few years earlier to form his own faction. The other suspects were mostly university and college students.

The continuation of bombings, even as the military accomplished such substantial gains in taking over a vast swath of the militant-controlled territories, underscored Pakistan's failure to formulate a comprehensive counterterrorism strategy and develop a strong intelligence network, or the kind of coordinated operations between the police, intelligence services, and military that could prevent attacks.

The military's success in Swat and South Waziristan also did not allay mounting pressure from the Obama administration to step up operations against the Afghan Taliban and their allies fighting the coalition forces across the border. The United States had been strenuously arguing that Pakistan must broaden its fight beyond the militants attacking its cities and security forces, and particularly stressed the importance of continuing the offensive into North Waziristan, the base of the powerful Haqqani network, which was a main perpetrator of attacks in Afghanistan. The Americans had placed a $200,000 bounty on the head of the network, Sirajuddin Haqqani, and considered breaking the back of the network's operations vital to success in the Afghan war. In August 2009 Maj. Gen. Curtis Scaparrotti, commander of the U.S. and NATO forces in eastern Afghanistan, told journalists that the Haqqani network was expanding its reach: "We've seen that expansion, and that's part of what we're fighting."[22] The following month an assessment delivered to the Obama administration by Gen. Stanley McChrystal, the commander of U.S. forces in Afghanistan, bluntly stated that the Afghan insurgency was "clearly supported from Pakistan," reportedly with aid from some elements of the ISI.[23]

Yet both the Pakistani government and the military had resisted all urging to launch operations against the network, further fueling U.S. speculation that the ISI had maintained its association with the Haqqanis from the time of the Afghan civil war for the purpose of exerting continued influence in

Afghanistan.[24] As President Obama reviewed the U.S. war strategy in Afghanistan in the fall of 2009, the launch of operations by Pakistani forces in North Waziristan became central to his planning, and also a central point of contention between the United States and Pakistan.

Negotiations were complicated by an outburst of outrage against the United States from the Pakistani public as well as the military in response to passage in late September of the Kerry-Lugar bill. Although it provided $1.5 billion of nonmilitary economic aid to Pakistan each year for the next five years, especially targeted at fighting the poverty in the tribal regions by funding development projects in energy, health, and education, the bill imposed strict conditions on the spending of the money. Among those conditions were stipulations that the Pakistani military make a significant commitment to stop militant attacks in Afghanistan, and specifically to take action against militants based in Quetta, widely considered the home base of the leader of the Afghan Taliban, Mullah Omar, as well as in the city of Muridke, near Lahore, which has been the main base of the militant group Lashkar-e-Taiba. The bill also required that the U.S. secretary of state verify, every six months, that the Pakistani military was still operating under the authority of the civilian government, a condition that clearly indicated the Americans' belief that the military was encroaching on that authority. Another controversial stipulation was that the United States be given "direct access to Pakistani nationals" who were suspected of being involved in nuclear proliferation, which reignited the issue of Pakistan's protection of the notorious nuclear scientist A. Q. Khan, who had confessed to sharing nuclear weapons secrets with Iran, North Korea, and Libya.[25]

The Kerry-Lugar bill, which was supported by the Zardari government, was widely perceived by Pakistanis as a lever for

U.S. control over their country, and most Pakistanis—the public, the military, the political opposition, and even members of the ruling coalition—vehemently protested the stipulations as a humiliating violation of Pakistani sovereignty. Just before the parliamentary debate on whether or not the government should agree to the bill's terms, the Pakistani military even took the unusual step—much to the embarrassment of the civilian government—of issuing a public statement expressing its concern. The military was most offended by language regarding the oversight of the civilian government concerning the promotion of military officers. General Kayani was so offended that he complained to the U.S. commander in Afghanistan, General McChrystal, when the two men met in Islamabad in October 2009.

The heated controversy threatened to drive a wedge of renewed distrust between the military and the civilian government and between the United States and Pakistan, just as so much headway was being made in the war against the militants and as increased cooperation between the U.S. military and Pakistani forces had so significantly aided in the advances made. Indeed some members of the government accused military intelligence of orchestrating a media campaign against the bill. Several senior opposition leaders and military officials even accused Hussain Haqqani, Pakistan's ambassador to Washington and a close aide to President Zardari, of deliberately getting the conditions inserted into the bill in order to humiliate the military. "I hope the whole thing is scrapped," one senior military official said. "At the very least we want it amended." [26]

The intensity of opposition, despite the huge increase in aid to be spent in the social sectors, shocked U.S. officials,[27] and the controversy threatened to throw President Obama's Pakistan policy into disarray even as he was formulating his new Af-Pak strategy. As the opposition swelled, President Zardari was forced to send his foreign minister, Shah Mahmood Qureshi, to Washington for discussions, and on October 14, 2009, Senator John Kerry issued a statement intended to alleviate the misgivings about the bill, which was outlined in an explanatory note attached to the bill. "There is no intent to, and nothing in this act in any way suggests that there should be, any U.S. role in micromanaging internal Pakistani affairs, including the promotion of Pakistani military officers or the internal operations of the Pakistani military," he said.[28]

Kerry's statement did little to quell the anger, however, and on October 28 U.S. Secretary of State Hillary Clinton traveled to Pakistan in an effort to to diffuse the tension. Militants greeted her arrival with a massive car bomb that day in a congested bazaar in Peshawar, a blast that killed 118 people, the bloodiest attack yet on civilians. Clinton promised to "turn a new page" in the testy relationship by broadening its focus beyond security issues, and she unleashed a charm offensive, making a number of public appearances. But she was greeted by harsh criticism in the Pakistani media.

In her appearances she was also directly confronted with the intensity of anger toward U.S. policy that had built up over many years. At a televised town hall meeting in Islamabad, a woman in the audience characterized U.S. drone missile strikes on suspected terrorist targets in northwestern Pakistan as "de facto acts of terrorism." "Is it the killing of innocent people in, let's say, drone attacks? Or is it the killing of innocent people in different parts of Pakistan, like the bomb blast in Peshawar two days ago? Which one is terrorism, do you think?" the woman asked.[29] Clinton faced similar questions at all of her appearances, from university students, journalists, and members of the civilian government. During an interview with several prominent female TV anchors before a predominantly female audience of several hundred, one member of the audience said the Predator attacks amount to "executions without trial" for those killed. During another meeting, with a group of tribesmen, Clinton was again put on the defensive. One tribesman told her, "Your presence in the region is not good for peace."[30]

Of course, her visit to Pakistan was not all about public relations. The Obama administration realized that the balance of power in the country had shifted considerably to the military, which was effectively running national security and foreign policy by this time, but was also extending its influence into other areas of the government. In a meeting that lasted more than three hours, in which General Kayani left no doubt that the army was calling the shots, Clinton tried to convince him that the United States was not seeking to undermine the army's authority.[31]

In the wake of the controversy over the Kerry-Lugar bill President Obama sent U.S. National Security Advisor Gen. James Jones to Islamabad for deliberations with Pakistan's civilian and military leadership. The former supreme commander of NATO arrived on November 13, just hours before the attack on the ISI office in Peshawar. He reportedly told Pakistani officials that President Obama would not view the border dividing Pakistan and Afghanistan as a barrier if he was responding to strikes emanating from Pakistan, which occurred almost daily. The message was clear: the United States expected the Pakistani military to expand and reorient its fight against the insurgency and target the Afghan Taliban and al Qaeda more vigorously. Jones particularly stressed that Pakistan should immediately move against the Haqqani network. The general did not impress the Pakistani leaders with his diplomatic skills. In referring to a meeting between Jones and Kayani, a senior

Pakistani official described the message delivered by Jones as a threat. "It was a testy meeting," he added.[32]

General Jones also delivered a letter from President Obama to President Zardari urging him to rally the nation's political and national security institutions in a united campaign to more intensively move against the extremists. He promised a range of new incentives to the Pakistanis, including enhanced intelligence sharing and military cooperation.[33]

The increased pressure failed, however, to convince the Pakistani forces to launch operations in North Waziristan. According to a senior Pakistani army official, it would have been disastrous to open another front without first consolidating the military's hold in the Swat Valley and South Waziristan. "It is not the Americans, but Pakistani military who should decide when to start [a] North Waziristan operation," he told me.[34] Pakistan also had serious reservations about the new Afghan strategy, which were conveyed to the U.S. administration in a letter drafted by General Kayani's office rather than the Foreign Ministry. The letter was meant to send a clear signal that the civilian government had virtually no say any longer in the county's national security affairs, and also in relations with Washington.[35]

Pakistan's primary concern regarding Obama's decision to send thirty thousand more troops to Afghanistan was that the surge would inevitably push many Taliban fighters across the border into Pakistan, which would threaten the gains that had been made in the Swat and South Waziristan offensives. There was also a strong belief in the military and the intelligence establishment that America's commitment to the region was waning and strong criticism that the new U.S. policy failed to offer a viable long-term political solution to the Afghan crisis. Without a stable government in Afghanistan before U.S.

withdrawal, they feared, there would be disastrous consequences for Pakistan, with Afghanistan becoming once again a proxy battleground for a struggle among the regional powers, including Iran and India. "Afghanistan will go back to a civil war with serious consequences for Pakistan," said a senior military official.[36]

In laying out his new strategy on November 30 at West Point, President Obama addressed those concerns. "In the past, we too often defined our relationship with Pakistan narrowly. Those days are over," he declared, directly addressing Pakistan.[37] But his words did little to reassure Pakistani officials that the United States had a reliable plan for stabilizing the hold on power of a legitimate government in Afghanistan.

In December 2009 the Obama administration authorized further expansion of the CIA's drone campaign, and U.S. officials said they might extend the strikes to the western province of Balochistan, in the Pakistani mainland, the capital city of which was the Afghan Taliban stronghold of Quetta.[38] The announcement provoked intense anger in the Pakistani military leadership, which declared that it would not allow any such U.S. incursion into the mainland. A major fear was that drone attacks on Quetta would destroy the fragile national consensus in Pakistan for the fight against the militants. The already strained relations between the countries had reached a new level of tension.

CHAPTER 8

The Scorpion's Tail

Confidence in the ability of the U.S. operations in Afghanistan to achieve control over the insurgency there was further shaken on December 30, 2009, when a suicide bomber blew himself up inside a remote CIA installation, Forward Operating Base Chapman, in Khost, on the border of North Waziristan. Seven CIA officers were killed. The attack was one of the worst in history against U.S. intelligence officials, and the infiltration of such a high-security facility was shocking. The bomber was later revealed to be a thirty-six-year-old Jordanian doctor, Humam Khalil Abu-Mulal al-Balawi, who had been recruited by Jordanian intelligence officials. He had convinced the CIA that he would bring them valuable intelligence on al Qaeda operations.[1]

In the first week of January 2010 Baitullah Mehsud's successor as chief of the Pakistani TTP, Hakimullah Mehsud, released a videotape of himself sitting with the bomber, which was apparently shot several days before the attack. On the tape Hakimullah vowed to take revenge for Baitullah's killing. The attack underscored that as effective as the CIA's drone operation had been against the militants, the groups retained the ability to carry out highly sophisticated and ever more audacious attacks.

The investigation of the attack on the Chapman base also offered detailed proof of closer collaboration between the TTP and al Qaeda. In early March U.S. intelligence officials revealed that one of the alleged planners of the attack was Hussein al-Yemeni, identified as one of al Qaeda's top twenty leaders, who was killed in a drone strike on March 8. In keeping with long-standing practice, the officials spoke on the condition of anonymity because the CIA formally declines to acknowledge U.S. participation in attacks inside Pakistani territory.[2]

A closer alliance between the TTP and al Qaeda had reportedly followed a meeting between Baitullah and Ayman al-Zawahiri in South Waziristan in 2008.[3] Until then the TTP had answered to the Afghan Taliban, but al Qaeda had come to exert more influence, and the TTP had begun to embrace al Qaeda's message of expanded, global jihad. The first evidence that the TTP was committed to operations outside of Pakistan and Afghanistan had emerged in January 2008, when Spanish authorities arrested twelve Pakistanis in connection with a terrorist plot in Barcelona. The plotters were discovered to have been in contact with Baitullah, and a spokesman for the TTP claimed the group's responsibility for the plot, saying that it was in response to Spain's military presence in Afghanistan.

In the wake of the Chapman base bombing, the Pakistani government supported an intensification of the CIA's drone campaign, and the strained relations between the countries took a turn for the better. In the two weeks following the December 30 bombing the CIA unleashed a hailstorm of drone attacks in North Waziristan. On January 12 a strike hit a suspected hideout of Hakimullah, a religious school in the area of Pasalkot, killing twelve people who were alleged to be militants. Hakimullah was injured but managed to escape.[4]

As the intensified drone campaign continued, the United States argued that the strikes were crippling the operational capabilities of the insurgents. It was in the wake of this series of successful strikes that CIA director Leon Panetta announced on March 17 that the drones had thrown al Qaeda into disarray. In a message intercepted by the CIA, one of Osama bin Laden's lieutenants was heard pleading to bin Laden to come to lead them. "It's pretty clear from all the intelligence we are getting," Panetta said, "that they are having a very difficult time putting together any kind of command and control, that they are scrambling. And that we really do have them on the run."[5] He credited their success to improved cooperation from the Pakistani government in identifying the targets.

Relations between the United States and Pakistan were further improved when the Obama administration offered hope of a more robust, nuanced approach to strengthening the relationship. In March high-level Pakistani officials of both the military and the civilian government flew to Washington for a strategic dialogue. The delegation was led by Foreign Minister Shah Mahmood Qureshi but was dominated by the army chief Gen. Ashfaq Kayani. The Americans were represented by Secretary of State Hillary Clinton and National Security Advisor James Jones, as well as additional senior military leaders. This was deemed the most important set of strategic meetings held between the two administrations to date. The Obama administration had scheduled the talks as part of a strategy to more vigorously support development initiatives in Pakistan, such as improvements in education, power generation, and trade, and to enhance the country's defense capabilities. "It's not the kind of commitment that you easily produce overnight or even within a year," Clinton declared. "But it is important to get started, to sort it out, and to develop the trust and the confidence between us."[6] Pakistani officials touted the meeting as a great success in increasing cooperation.

The countries pledged to set the relations between them on a more solid footing, moving beyond the Bush administration's almost exclusive focus on military aid and cooperation to a new emphasis on economic and social sector development in Pakistan. Since 2001 the United States had given Pakistan more than $11 billion in aid, which had helped prop up the country's faltering economy. But a large part of that money had gone to financing Pakistan's military campaign against the militants, which hadn't even begun to cover the total cost of those operations. Pakistani and international aid agencies believed that, in total, the war on terror had cost Pakistan's economy more than $35 billion.

Washington now agreed to provide help in building power-generation capacity, such as dams, as well as other infrastructure. Additional military assistance was pledged as well, including the delivery of F-16 fighter planes. That pledge went a long way to mollify the anger in the military caused by the stringent conditions attached to the Kerry-Lugar bill.

The improvement in relations was derailed just months later, however, when Pakistani-born Faisal Shahzad attempted to detonate a car bomb in Times Square, in the heart of New York City. Shahzad's story followed a now familiar narrative. Like so many of the newer recruits to the militant cause, he was middle class, educated, and angry with the U.S. occupations of Iraq and Afghanistan and with the CIA's drone raids. "They shouldn't be shooting people from the sky. You know, they should come down and fight," he had told his Connecticut neighbor Dennis Flanner a year before the attempted bombing.[7]

The son of a retired vice marshal in the Pakistani Air Force, Shahzad seemed to have attained all that a Pakistani youth could aspire to. He had moved to the United States, and after earning his college degree found a good job at the global cosmetic firm Elizabeth Arden. By 2004 he was married to an American of Pakistani origin and had two children. He owned a home in New Jersey and had become an American citizen in April 2009. There had been no indication that he was involved with militant Islam until he was arrested; his family was not in any way extremist, and he had no background in Islamist schooling. His turn to extremism had happened in the United States, and it caused such strains in his marriage that his wife moved to Saudi Arabia with their children in June 2009 to live with her parents.[8]

Shahzad traced the origin of his plot to a 2009 trip he made to Pakistan, just three months after becoming a U.S. citizen. While staying with his parents he met a number of radicalized young men much like himself, in Karachi and Islamabad. One of those he came into contact with was the American-educated son of the owner of one of Pakistan's biggest catering companies, Rajput Caterers, which regularly arranged parties at U.S. Embassy functions. Salman Ashraf was picked up by Pakistani intelligence agents from Islamabad a few days after the bombing attempt. His family professed no knowledge of any involvement on his part in terrorist activities. "He was a hard working boy who had nothing to do with militancy," his elderly father told a Pakistani television network.[9] Ahmed Reza, a business partner of Salman Ashraf, was another suspect linked to Shahzad. In his mid-thirties, he was picked up by intelligence operatives while driving back to his home in Islamabad. Neither Reza nor Ashraf have been produced before any court of law or charged.

Another of those suspected of assisting Shahzad was Mohammed Shahid. In his early thirties, he had earned a college degree in business in the United States. Though his family was devoutly religious, there was no known history of their involvement in any extremist activities. The intelligence agencies believed Shoib Mughul, a young computer designer, was the man who helped Shahzad make contact with the Taliban. He was also picked up in the sweep. Shahid and Mughul were suspected of operating as an informal network that helped to recruit Pakistanis living abroad who wanted to return home to train for terrorist attacks.[10] They later confessed before a court to having facilitated Shahzad's travel to Waziristan and his meeting with the Taliban leaders. They were also charged with planning terrorist attacks in Pakistan.

For some time the Obama administration had been concerned that the TTP, acting in collaboration with al Qaeda, had developed a global agenda and was setting its sights on attacks in the United States. Those concerns had intensified when, on December 30, 2009, the same day as the Chapman base bombing, five young Muslim American friends living in the Washington, D.C., suburbs—Umar Farooq, twenty-four, Waqar Khan, twenty-two, Ramy Zamzam, twenty-two, Ahmed Minni, twenty, and Aman Hassan Yemer, eighteen— were arrested in the town of Sargodha, southwest of Islamabad, where Umar Farooq had family connections. They had made contact by email with a militant commander, Qari Saifullah, who said he would take them to the tribal region, but they were arrested before they made the trip. The police asserted that they were planning to carry out terrorist attacks.[11]

The Americans admitted to the police that they wanted to go to Afghanistan to join the jihad against the U.S. forces, but later retracted their statement, telling the court that they were on a humanitarian mission and wanted to help Afghani victims of the war. On June 24, 2010, they were each sentenced to ten years in prison in Pakistan on counts of funding outlawed organizations and conspiracy to commit crimes and terrorism in Pakistan. Other charges, of conspiracy to commit terrorism in Afghanistan and the United States, were dropped due to a lack of evidence.[12]

Their reported plans to receive training in al Qaeda camps, and the story of Faisal Shahzad's path to his attempted bombing, were chilling confirmation that extremists were planning attacks within the United States. Shahzad reportedly traveled to North Waziristan with an activist of the outlawed militant group Jaish-e-Mohammed whom he met in Karachi. He was said to have met with TTP leaders there and to have received training in bomb making. The TTP surely deemed a radicalized American national a great catch, and they were quick to claim responsibility for the plot, releasing an audiotape two days later in which Qari Hussain said that the attempt was "revenge for the Global American interference and terrorism in Muslim countries, especially in Pakistan."[13] He referred in particular to the killings of Baitullah Mehsud and the former leader of the al Qaeda Islamic State of Iraq, Abu Omar al Baghdadi, by Iraqi forces in mid-April 2009. Shahzad echoed those words when, on June 22, after confessing to the attempt, he told the judge ruling on his case, "The drone hits in Afghanistan and Iraq, they don't see children, they don't see anybody. They kill women, children, they kill everybody. They're killing all Muslims." He said he was avenging those attacks. "I am part of the answer to the U.S. terrorizing the Muslim nations and the Muslim people."[14]

In July a videotape of Shahzad in tribal dress showed him embracing Hakimullah Mehsud in Waziristan. The footage, aired on the al Arabia TV network, confirmed Shahzad's close links with the Taliban. The meeting apparently took place just before the Pakistani Army launched a major offensive against Hakimullah's Taliban forces in South Waziristan in October

2009. In a video message recorded after the meeting Shahzad vowed to avenge the killing of Baitullah.

The bombing attempt alarmed the Obama administration and significantly undermined the progress that had been made in the improvement of relations between Pakistan and the United States in recent months.[15] Gen. James Jones and Leon Panetta traveled to Islamabad in the second week of May 2010 to deliver a stern message to Pakistani leaders. They had brought with them a dossier with details about Shahzad's contacts with Pakistani militants, and they warned that there would be serious consequences for Pakistan if there were another attack in the United States traceable to their country.[16]

They further stipulated that Pakistan had only weeks to show real progress in a crackdown on the group allegedly behind the attempt. "It was almost like reading a riot act to Pakistani leaders," said a Pakistani official familiar with the talks. Pakistan responded to the warning by rounding up suspects who were believed to be in contact with Shahzad; however, they were never charged or tried by any court of law. Pakistani security officials nevertheless claimed the crackdown broke apart the network affiliated with the Taliban.

Further strain in the relations occurred when the Obama administration pressured President Zardari to allow more U.S. operations within Pakistan. The Times Square bombing attempt had convinced the Americans that the targeted killing of militants by the drone strikes was insufficient to stem the tide of the insurgency and that an expanded U.S. military presence on the ground in Pakistan was required.[17] The United States assured Pakistan that the additional troops would serve only as advisors and trainers and would not engage in combat. The Americans also demanded improvement in real-time intelligence sharing, including access to flight data for all passengers flying out of Pakistan, and asked to establish an intelligence outpost in Quetta, the alleged headquarters of the Afghan Taliban. U.S. intelligence had already been operating such an outpost on the outskirts of Peshawar in northwestern Pakistan. These measures were intended not only to prevent any possible terrorist attack in the United States originating from Pakistan, but also to monitor Pakistan's campaign against the militants.[18]

The meetings in May represented the Obama administration's toughest talk yet to the Pakistani leadership, a reflection of the widespread perception that America's Pakistan problem appeared to have gotten worse, not better, on President Obama's watch. The officials did not spell out what action the United States might take if Pakistan did not comply, but Pakistani officials were concerned that the Americans might launch a unilateral ground strike on the tribal areas. That apprehension was fueled by a television interview with Secretary of State Clinton after the Times Square bombing attempt in which she declared, "If, heaven forbid, an attack like this that we can trace back to Pakistan were to have been successful, there would be very severe consequences."[19]

The demands were extremely difficult for Islamabad to comply with, as they would surely cause serious political fallout. The military refused to allow additional U.S. troops but agreed to increase intelligence cooperation. The American military presence in Pakistan had already grown substantially over the past year. More than two hundred troops were involved in a program to share intelligence with the Pakistani Army and paramilitary troops and to train them to battle militants in the northwestern region. Some U.S. troops had also accompanied Pakistani paramilitary forces in the field as observers. The presence of U.S. troops was such a politically explosive issue in Pakistan that the troops were not allowed out of military areas. The government had never publicly acknowledged their presence.

Pakistani officials were also unhappy that the visit by Jones and Panetta had gone ahead despite requests from the Foreign Ministry and the military that at least Panetta should not be a part of the high-profile visit. In a show of protest the ISI chief, Gen. Ahmed Shuja Pasha, excused himself from meeting the officials on the pretext of illness. Doing so "sent a wrong signal," a senior Pakistani official said.[20]

The military felt particularly uneasy with the aggressive tone of Clinton's message and with the intensified pressure for the launch of a ground offensive in North Waziristan. Washington argued that Pakistan was still not doing enough to counter the insurgents there, and in particular continued to avoid taking on the Haqqani network. The Pakistani Army's willingness to move on North Waziristan and the network had become a litmus test for relations between Islamabad and Washington, and the two sides were at an increasingly tension-ridden impasse. The difference in views was representative of a larger divide in perceptions about Washington's new Af-Pak strategy. The first major operation carried out according to the new surge strategy had done nothing to instill greater confidence within the Pakistani military of the ultimate success of the strategy.

The much publicized military offensive in the Marjah district of Afghanistan's Helmand province was launched on February 13, 2010, with the aim of removing all Taliban forces from the city. The operation, named Moshtrak, was a NATO-Afghan joint offensive involving fifteen thousand troops backed by combat helicopters and fighter jets, and it constituted the largest joint operation of the war up to that point. The offensive was a crucial test for President Obama's new strategy. Unlike in previous offensives, in which territory won from the Taliban was later abandoned, the troops planned to clear the area and hold it for as long as it took to establish a functional local security system and government. Afghan and international civilian officials were to be moved into the district once fighting was over to carry out development work, for which the money was already available.

General Jones told Fox News in an interview just days before the start of the Marjah operation, "What's important about this operation is that it is the first major operation in which we will demonstrate, I think successfully, that the new elements of the strategy—which combine not only security operations but economic reform and good governance at the local and regional level with a much more visible presence of Afghan forces—will take place." He continued, "[A] successfully demonstrated and executed operation [in Marjah] is going to make a big change in not only the southern part of Afghanistan, but will send shock waves through the rest of the country that there is a new direction, there's a new commitment." [21]

The first days of battle went well for the NATO and Afghan forces. They encountered heavy resistance from the Taliban but succeeded in forcing the insurgents to retreat after two weeks of fighting. As the battle raged on, though, the intensity of the fighting increased, and the coalition started to suffer heavy casualties from both improvised bombs and Taliban sniper fire. The NATO forces were able to establish firm control only over the three bazaars that make up Marjah's commercial centers, while the Taliban roamed relatively freely throughout the rest of the city. The coalition forces declared the operation culminated on February 25, 2010, after hoisting the Afghan flag in the area, and a U.S. commander declared that most combat operations had halted, although the coalition forces would still need several weeks to exert control over more remote villages. [22] But establishing a suitable local government that could win over an alienated population proved too great a challenge, and doing so was crucial to the success of the offensive. Before long the Taliban fighters simply melted back into the population. Many of them slipped into crews that came to work the poppy harvest. Others had never left their villages and had just lain low during the operation. Gradually they found ways to operate once again, moving in small groups, attacking the coalition troops, and threatening to kill anyone who cooperated with the Americans.[23] Ultimately neither the American forces nor the Taliban could gain the upper hand, and they reached an uneasy standoff with almost daily clashes.

The difficulties in Marjah are indicative of the enormous challenges of eliminating a deeply rooted insurgency. General McChrystal had predicted that once security was established in Marjah a "government in a box" could be swiftly installed. But there was hardly any government in place even months after the operation was declared concluded. A U.S. Senate hearing in May 2010 offered a grim assessment of the state of Marjah, almost three months after the operation was declared over. Senator John Kerry, chairman of the Senate Foreign Relations Committee, said Marjah did not appear to be the turning point it was meant to be in the overall mission in Afghanistan. "A recent survey conducted by the International Council on Security and Development showed that a vast majority of villagers felt negatively about foreign troops and that more young Afghans had joined the Taliban over the last year," he said at the hearing.[24]

The Obama administration had declared July 2011 as the date for the commencement of U.S. withdrawal from Afghanistan. Now, in the middle of 2010, the coalition forces were left with only six months to make decisive progress, and that prospect was looking increasingly unrealistic. The Karzai government has yet to show any progress in providing good governance and bringing down corruption, and Afghanistan has virtually become a narcostate. According to one estimate, the Taliban has reestablished a strong presence in 75 percent of the country's districts. The insurgency has also continued to spread, expanding even to non-Pashtun areas. Plans for a major offensive on the Taliban stronghold of Kandahar, Afghanistan's second biggest city, were delayed due to the military's inability to gain the support of the local population for the operation. And in the meantime American casualties kept rising.

Pakistani officials have been deeply concerned about what they perceive as disarray in the U.S. Afghan policy. "After nine years of war the U.S. led mission is mired in confusion and uncertainty," said Maleeha Lodhi, a former Pakistani ambassador to Washington. "The unresolved tension in American strategy has now caught up."[25] The assumption behind the July 2011 deadline was that the Karzai government and the Afghani security forces and military would be prepared to take over the primary responsibilities for security by that time. Pakistani officials deem that possibility simply unrealistic.

The Obama administration has argued that the deadline was necessary to force President Karzai to improve his governance of his country, but that thinking ignored the reality of the political situation in Afghanistan. Karzai's political standing was seriously eroded by accusations of corruption in the October 2009 elections, including allegations of widespread poll rigging involving his close family members. In addition, his own brother was accused of being involved in drug trafficking. Karzai's relations with the Obama administration have also become severely strained. So bad has the situation become that special envoy Richard Holbrooke and Karzai have stopped talking to each other. Karzai's relations with his other Western allies, particularly Britain, have also become quite frosty.

The expectation that the Afghan military and police would be able to take over primary control within that timeframe was also highly dubious. A key part of the strategy was the training of Afghani military and police forces. But building a professional and competent army and police force has proved to be much harder than American officials had anticipated. The United States has spent more than $6 billion since 2002 to create an effective Afghan National Police (ANP) force, supplying weapons, building police academies, and hiring defense contractors to train the recruits. But the program has been a disaster. Fewer than 12 percent of the country's police units are capable of operating on their own. Police commanders have been implicated in drug trafficking, and Richard Holbrooke has publicly called the ANP "an inadequate organization, riddled with corruption." The public's distrust of the police was palpable during the Marjah operation, when the village elders told the Americans that they did not want the ANP to return.[26]

The training of the military has also gone off the rails. U.S. Defense Secretary Robert Gates admitted that the coalition was short of the number of trainers needed to expand the Afghan National Army. According to the reports, morale in the army remains low, illiteracy is high, and the rate of defection continues to increase. The Pentagon has authorized a substantial increase in the number of Afghan security forces it plans to train by October 2011, in time for the planned beginning of withdrawal, and the new goal would increase the size of the Afghan National Army from 102,400 personnel to 171,600. A pay raise of 30 percent was also instituted in the effort to get more Afghans to join.[27] But American officials acknowledge that serious difficulties in training persist. The obstacles were outlined in a recent series of internal administration reviews that described the Afghan Army and police as largely illiterate, often corrupt, and poorly led. Widespread use of marijuana, opium, and heroin among troops is also a serious problem.[28]

A report on the Afghan Army by the International Crisis Group, a Brussels-based think tank, described a force riven by ethnic and political divisions and plagued by corruption: "As a result, the army is a fragmented force, serving disparate interests, and far from attaining the unified national character needed to confront numerous security threats."[29]

In Afghanistan the United States faces many of the same problems that the Pakistani military has contended with in Waziristan and the other tribal regions. The military operations there have also failed to deliver a decisive victory, largely because a weak civilian administration was unable to establish its authority in the conflict zones. A major concern among the Pakistani security establishment has been that the worsening disarray in Afghanistan will have further serious destabilizing effects on Pakistan. Pakistani military officials are particularly alarmed at the prospect of the entire region of Pakistan and Afghanistan turning into a battleground.[30]

With such a prospect looming, the Pakistani military is simply unwilling to launch a major operation in North Waziristan. "We cannot start the operation on the U.S. pressure. We have our own priorities," said a senior Pakistani army official.[31] Pakistan still has more than sixty thousand troops engaged in combat duties in South Waziristan, the Swat Valley, and the Orakzai, Khyber, and Bajaur tribal regions, and the military is already badly stretched. "We cannot leave these areas unsettled and open another front," said the official. To combat the estimated ten thousand highly trained and motivated guerrillas commanded by the Haqqani network, Pakistan would need to deploy fifty thousand to sixty thousand additional troops.

The deep reluctance to take action against the Haqqani network is also a reflection of Pakistan's worries about the events that will follow the eventual American pullout from Afghanistan. The military is convinced that when U.S. troops leave, a renewed civil war will break out. In that scenario the Pashtun-dominated Afghan Taliban and the Haqqani network could be used once again by Pakistan as a proxy force for exercising control over the Afghan government and countering Indian influence in Afghanistan.

Disagreements between the United States and Pakistan about the situation in Afghanistan and the likely outcome of the U.S. military operations there have become the central point of contention in the complex and tense relationship. In light of the concerns about what will follow the U.S. pullout, in February 2010 General Kayani warned that Pakistan's strategic interests must be served in any future political arrangement in Afghanistan. "A friendly Afghanistan can provide Pakistan strategic depth," he declared.[32]

These concerns have made General Kayani receptive to the possibility of working with the Karzai government to broker a peace settlement. Given the chaos in U.S. policy and the chasm that has opened up between his government and the United States, Karzai has lately shown a degree of autonomy that has caused great concern in Washington. In particular, he has begun pursuing his own policy of reconciliation in the war, seeking to build bridges to the Taliban. In early January 2010 the president's brother, Ahmed Wali Karzai, reportedly held two secret meetings with Mullah Abdul Ghani Baradar, a deputy to the Taliban's supreme leader, Mullah Omar, in Spin Boldak, a town on the border with Pakistan.[33] Mullah Baradar has been credited with rebuilding the Taliban into an effective fighting force and running the group's day-to-day affairs for many years, with Mullah Omar taking a backseat because of his failing health. Besides heading the Taliban's military operations, he reportedly also ran the group's leadership council, known as the Quetta Shura. The meeting with him was reportedly the first major contact of the Karzai government with the senior Taliban leadership.[34] Karzai's reconciliation efforts have been known to American officials, but have not had their approval.

Just weeks after the meeting, Mullah Baradar was arrested in Karachi in a joint operation by U.S. and Pakistani intelligence services. He was believed to have been traveling often to Karachi, and up to that point he and other Afghan Taliban leaders had moved freely around the country for years. The Pakistani security forces could have arrested him at any time, and his arrest so soon after the meeting was highly suggestive. Some reports asserted that the arrest was the result of infighting within the Taliban. Mullah Baradar's contacts with Karzai did not seem to have the approval of Mullah Omar or the Taliban leadership council, and it is quite plausible that his arrest was consented to by the insurgent leadership. A senior Pakistani intelligence officer involved in the operation indicated that Baradar had received funding and weapons from Iran. The Iranian link was a serious cause for concern for the Pakistani security establishment, particularly as Tehran has traditionally supported the Afghan Northern Alliance. It also reinforced the suspicion that Iran was seeking to make some inroads into the insurgent movement to maintain its influence in Afghanistan.

Whatever the precipitating cause of the arrest, while the capture of one the highest ranking insurgent commanders was hailed by Washington as a great success, Hamid Karzai was livid. He believed the action was a deliberate move to undermine the negotiations he had started.[35] The arrest, however, did not distract him from the reconciliation efforts, and he kept channels open to other insurgent leaders, such as Gulbuddin Hekmatyar.

Given Karzai's olive branch to the Taliban, the Obama administration is faced with a very difficult question: whether or not to reconcile with insurgent commanders who continue to have close ties with al Qaeda. The administration is clearly divided on the issue of when and how to open negotiations with the Taliban. Officially the Pentagon has been skeptical about opening talks with high-ranking Taliban leaders anytime soon. "It's our view that until the Taliban leadership sees a change in the momentum and begins to see that they are not going to win, the likelihood of significant reconciliation at senior levels is not terribly great," Defense Secretary Gates said in January 2010.[36]

But while negotiations with Mullah Omar and other hardcore Taliban leaders have been completely ruled out, when it became apparent that the war would not be won purely on the battlefield, American officials privately acknowledged that they were considering the idea of talks with lower ranking insurgents. The senior American commander in Afghanistan, General McChrystal, even said that he could envision an eventual role for some Taliban officials in Afghanistan's political establishment. But officials also warned that the plan was rife with political risks. Negotiations with the Taliban leadership could jeopardize any plans to reconcile and reintegrate lower ranking Taliban fighters back into Afghan society.[37]

While the Karzai government has accused the Pakistani military and the ISI of continuing to support Taliban insurgents with training and logistics, the Pakistani security establishment has worried about the increasing closeness of the Kabul regime, which is dominated by the non-Pashtun Northern Alliance, to India. With the prospect of the U.S. pullout looming, the proxy war between Islamabad and Delhi over influence in Afghanistan has heated up. India has been able to expand its influence because of its long ties with the Northern Alliance, and is also deeply involved in development work in Afghanistan. Pakistan has tried to hamper India's efforts to expand its influence by supporting two bomb attacks on the Indian Embassy in Kabul, both reportedly carried out by the Haqqani network, and reportedly with the aid of the ISI.[38] In the most deadly attack, on July 7, 2008, a suicide bomber rammed his explosives-packed vehicle into the embassy, killing fifty-four people, including an Indian defense attaché. In another attack, on October 8, 2009, a car packed with explosives blew up beside the Indian Embassy, killing seventeen people. American intelligence officials concluded within weeks that the ISI had helped to plan that attack, though Pakistan denied any involvement.[39]

But with Karzai initiating talks with the Taliban, the Pakistani military has perceived an opening for establishing its influence over the situation in Afghanistan, especially given its continuing ties to some of the insurgent groups, including the Haqqani network. That opening seemed to widen when, in June, Karzai fired his interior minister, Hanif Atmar, and the powerful intelligence chief, Amrullah Saleh. Both, but particularly Saleh, were opposed to any reconciliation with the Taliban. They had both fought against the Taliban as part of the Northern Alliance forces during the Afghan civil war. For the same reason they were also known to have anti-Pakistani views. Pakistan had been pressing Karzai for a long time to remove them from their posts in order to facilitate better relations between Kabul and Islamabad. "They were great obstacles in the way of any meaningful cooperation between the two countries, particularly on the security issues," said a senior Pakistani intelligence official. But Karzai had long resisted, in part because the two were highly regarded in Washington. They had worked closely with the American forces since the invasion of Afghanistan in October 2001, and the Obama administration strongly objected to their unceremonious firing. Pentagon spokesman Geoff Morrell said both officials were "people we admire and whose service we appreciate." [40]

Pursuing this side channel of possible negotiations with the Taliban, General Kayani and ISI chief Lt. Gen. Shuja Pasha made a number of trips to Kabul in mid-2010, arguing that they could deliver Sirajuddin Haqqani's involvement in a future power-sharing arrangement. No direct meeting between Sirajuddin and Afghan officials followed, however; a senior Pakistani official said the talks were conducted through emissaries and that there was no major breakthrough. According to Maj. Gen. Athar Abbas, the chief spokesman for the Pakistani military, the United States was well aware of what was going on. "Gen. McChrystal was present in every meeting between Gen. Kayani and Karzai," he said. [41]

Washington has watched this evolving partnership with serious concern and distrusts the notion that the Haqqani network will act in good faith as a power broker. Reacting to Pakistan's efforts to broker the talks, President Obama said, "I think we have to view these efforts with skepticism but also with openness." [42] But CIA chief Leon Panetta was more forceful in expressing doubts about the Haqqanis' intent. "We have seen no evidence that they are truly interested in reconciliation, where they would surrender their arms, where they would denounce al Qaeda, where they would really try to become part of the society," he said. [43]

A central issue regarding any brokering of a power-sharing agreement by the Haqqanis is whether they can be reliably separated from al Qaeda, to which they are closely linked. Some Pakistani intelligence officials believe that the Haqqanis can be persuaded to cut their ties with al Qaeda if there is a clear indication of a peace deal that will pave the way for the coalition forces to leave Afghanistan. But there are also serious doubts that the Haqqanis can really make a deal with Karzai given their close ties to the Taliban, and that the Karzai government relies so heavily on U.S. support.

The discussions have also generated a new uncertainty among the anti-Taliban forces within Afghanistan, seen by the leaders of the minority ethnic communities as an attempt to reestablish Pashtun domination. This development has not only further threatened Karzai's own survival in power, but has reignited the ethnic and regional polarization that prevailed in the country during the chaos of the 1990s.

In addition Pakistan's move to broker a deal with the Haqqani network reignited tensions with the United States over the long-time allegations of Pakistan's continued patronage of some Afghan Taliban factions. Secretary of State Clinton said in July 2010 that elements in Pakistan's security agencies knew the whereabouts of Osama bin Laden, and she again warned of serious consequences if any attack on the United States was traced back to Pakistan. The tension over that issue was also greatly intensified by the posting in late July of some ninety-two thousand classified U.S. documents about the war in Afghanistan on the Wikileaks website. Mostly raw intelligence reports, the documents illustrate in vivid detail why the nine-year-long war, which has already cost the United States almost $300 billion, has gone so badly and why the Taliban are stronger than at any time since 2001. Spanning five years, from January 2004 to 2009, the reports have also substantiated what had already been widely understood about the continued relationship between the Afghan Taliban and the ISI.

A more shocking revelation, though, was that the Taliban fighters have used portable heat-seeking missiles against coalition aircraft, the same weapons that helped the Mujahideen win the war against the Soviet forces.[44] A major question is who supplied the Taliban with these weapons this time around. The documents also reveal that rising civilian casualties in Afghanistan due to air bombings have turned the public increasingly against the U.S.-led forces, and that the drone strikes, which the American forces have increasingly used against targets in Afghanistan, have been far less effective than has been officially portrayed.

Even as the United States pushes ahead with the surge strategy in Afghanistan, the view is becoming more widespread that the war is unwinnable. The resilience of the insurgency has become ever more clear, and despite the assertion by CIA chief Panetta that al Qaeda has been decimated, the reality is that there is a new al Qaeda, composed largely of the new Pakistani recruits from the educated, urban middle class. Deeply ideologically committed, this new breed of militants is now spearheading the spreading war in Pakistan and also supporting the insurgents fighting the American forces across the border in Afghanistan.

With the growing radicalization of Muslim youth in the West, who receive inspiration from these new jihadists, more attempts like that of Shahzad to launch attacks on the United States, as well as targets around the world, are also to be expected. And with the growing sophistication of the terrorist network, the chances of a successful attack must be deemed quite high.

Conclusion

As the U.S. war in Afghanistan enters its tenth year—the longest war the United States has ever fought—there is no clear end in sight. What was started as a fight to overthrow the Taliban and hunt down al Qaeda forces has escalated into a wider regional conflict, with Afghanistan now the center of a new Great Game and Pakistan, India, and Iran vying for influence. These raised stakes, and the long neglect of the militants' resurgence while the West was focused on the war in Iraq, have transformed the conflict into a quagmire.

The Obama administration has endorsed a plan for the Afghan government to take responsibility for security in the country by 2014, and in a conference in Kabul on July 20, 2010, the United States and its allies in the war expressed optimism that the Afghan security forces would be ready to take over by that time. President Karzai vowed to curb the endemic corruption in the government, and U.S. Secretary of State Clinton said, "Now we must focus all our energies on making this vision a reality."

But the increasingly perilous situation on the ground offers little hope of achieving that objective. The expectation that the weak Karzai government will be able to transform Afghanistan into a viable state by 2014 is unrealistic at best.

The Taliban insurgents are much more powerful than at any time since their defeat in 2001. They are more organized and also now possess more sophisticated weaponry, as revealed by the Wikileaks documents. The surge in U.S. troops and President Obama's new counterinsurgency strategy have shown little sign of success. Indeed the Marjah operation revealed that the notion that a "government in a box" can be established in territory that has been secured is fundamentally flawed.

The Obama administration is still searching for a political strategy to complement the surge effort, and there are contradictory signals emanating from Washington about its goals in Afghanistan. That lack of a clear strategy indicates that Washington knows neither how to end the conflict nor how to continue an increasingly unpopular war that cannot be won. The administration is also losing public support for the war. In an extraordinary vote in Congress on July 27, 2010, on the allocation of an additional $437 billion of war funding, 114 members voted against, including 102 Democrats. This muddled approach has added to the confusion and widened the differences within the coalition.

In several European parliaments the mood is much the same. The Netherlands has already pulled out its troops from Afghanistan, and other NATO countries are under increasing pressure to follow suit.

Meanwhile in Pakistan an increasingly unpopular government mired in corruption is incapable of leading the nation at perhaps at the most critical point in its history. Having emerged from ten years of military rule with the ouster of President Musharraf, the country has descended into near chaos. President Zardari is fundamentally discredited, seen as slavishly pro-American, and the worsening economic situation has fueled growing discontent among the mainstream population, providing an ever more conducive environment for the continuing rise of militancy and religious extremism. The Islamists are gaining ground in the face of the abject failure of the civilian democratic institutions. And although the military has dealt a serious blow to the militants in their strongholds in the northwest, they are far from defeated and are continuing to launch shocking attacks in the major cities.

In the face of this threat and the ineptitude of the civilian government, the Pakistani military has been perpetrating a creeping coup, taking charge of the country's national security and foreign policy, a development that certainly does not bode well for the preservation of the democratic process. But even with the tightened military control, the rising terrorism targeting the urban centers and the unending war in FATA have dramatically deepened Pakistan's economic crisis and widened the already problematic social and ideological divides within the country. Pakistan has become a powder keg, and the fragmentation of the country has become a real possibility. The country may not be facing an imminent Islamic fundamentalist takeover, but there is a real danger that radical Islamists will seize control of some regions.

There have been two fundamental flaws in the approach to the war against the Islamic extremists in the region. One has been the failure to understand that this is so largely a Pashtun war, and that the Pashtuns in Pakistan would become so strongly allied with both al Qaeda and the Taliban. This is not a war in Afghanistan; it is a war in Afghanistan and Pakistan. The failure to appreciate the severity of the threat posed by the Pakistani militant groups was a failure not only of the United States but of the Musharraf government as well. The second fundamental flaw has been the failure to appreciate that combating the militant threat required something far more than a military campaign. It required—and still does—a comprehensive social and political plan, as well as strong political leadership. Both have been sorely lacking.

There is a growing realization among all parties that the war may not end in defeat for either side, but in some sort of political settlement with the insurgents, requiring direct talks with the Taliban. But the United States and its allies have not been able to reach a consensus on negotiations with the Taliban. This must become an urgent priority.

Many Western European nations have stressed the need for an immediate opening of dialogue with the insurgents, arguing that ending the war simply will not be possible without an internationally supported agreement with the Taliban. British Foreign Secretary David Miliband laid out a roadmap to negotiations with the Taliban in a speech at MIT in March 2010 that called for unconditional talks with all parties except for those committed to al Qaeda. "Dialogue is not appeasement," he said. But the Obama administration has not been prepared to move at that pace.

To be sure, a political settlement will be extremely difficult to achieve. There is even a question whether the Taliban is prepared at this point to talk. But the overarching lesson of the always regenerating insurgency, and the inability of both the coalition forces and the Pakistani forces to keep the militant groups from regrouping, is perfectly clear: a political settlement is the only endgame.

Notes

Introduction:

1 www.washingtontimes.com/news/2010/jul/14/shahzad-vows
-avenge-martyred-terrorists/.
2 CNN, August 10, 2009.; AFP, August 2009.
3 Author interview with a senior Pakistani Army officer, 2009; "Death of
Taliban Chief Blow to Extremists," MSNBC News Service, August 7,
2009.
4 "CIA Director says secret attacks in Pakistan have hobbled al-Qaeda,"
Washington Post, March 18, 2010. www.washingtonpost.com/wp-dyn/
content/article/2010/03/17/AR2010031702558.html.
5 "CIA's Silent War in Pakistan," *Time*, June 1, 2009.
6 *Wall Street Journal*, March 26, 2009.
7 abcnews.go.com/ThisWeek/cia-director-panetta-exclusive-intell
igence-bin-laden-location/story?id=11027374.
8 "More Than a One-Man Problem," *The Economist*, June 26, 2010.

Chapter 1:

1 Zahid Hussain, *Frontline Pakistan: The Struggle with Militant Islam* (New
York: Columbia University Press, 2007), 18.
2 news.bbc.co.uk/2/hi/programmes/correspondent/1682466.stm.
3 Ahmed Rashid, *Taliban* (London: I. B. Taurus, 2000), 186–87.
4 Author interview with Iftikhar Murshid, a former Pakistani special
envoy to Afghanistan, 2000.
5 Abou Zahab, "The Regional Dimension of Sectarian Conflict," in *Pakistan Nationalism Without a Nation*, ed. Christopher Jafferlot (London:
Zed Books, 2002), 120.

Notes

6 "In the Shadow of Terrorism," *Newsline* (Pakistan), February 2000.

7 Ibid.

8 "The New Frontier." *Newsline*, April 2004; author interview with Maleeha Lodhi, 2010.

9 Author interview with Atynia Bakar, Asia bureau chief of Al Arabia TV, 2008.

10 Hussain, *Frontline Pakistan*, 122.

11 Ahmed Rashid, *Descent into Chaos* (London: Allen Lane, 2008), 117.

12 "Al Qaeda's New Face," *Newsline*, August 2004.

13 www.time.com/time/nation/article/0,8599,436061,00.html.

14 news.bbc.co.uk/2/hi/south_asia/1818898.stm.

15 "The Mullah's Fight Back," *Newsline*, October 2002.

16 "Backward March," *Newsline*, July 2003.

17 Author interview with Maleeha Lodhi, Pakistan's former ambassador to Washington, 2008.

18 Author interview with a top Pakistani Army officer who had served in the ISI, 2010.

19 Pervez Musharraf, *In the Line of Fire* (New York: Free Press, 2006), 265.

20 "Amid U.S. Policy Dispute, Qaeda Grows in Pakistan," *New York Times*, June 30, 2008.

21 Associated Press, July 30, 2001.

22 www.criticalthreats.org/pakistan/survivalist-north-waziristan-hafiz -gul-bahadur-biography-and-analysis.

23 Ibid.

24 Steve Coll, *The Bin Ladens* (London: Allen Lane, 2008), 294.

25 Peter Bergen, "The Long Hunt for Osama," *Atlantic*, October 2004.

26 Author interview with the staff of the madrassa and local residents a few days after the raid in 2002.

27 NBC interview with Sirajuddin, July 29, 2008.

28 "Pakistan's Dangerous Double Game," *Newsweek*, September 13, 2008.

29 NBC interview with Sirajuddin, July 29, 2008.

30 "Afghan Strikes by Taliban Get Pakistan Help, U.S. Aides Say," *New York Times*, March 25, 2009.

31 Author interview with Maj. Gen. Athar Abbas and a former ISI officer, 2009.

Chapter 2:

1 Lawrence Ziring, *Pakistan at the Cross-current of History* (Pakistan: Vanguard Books, 2004), 42; www.time.com/time/printout/0,8816,854810,00 .html.

Notes

2 www.time.com/time/covers/0,16641,19471027,00.html.

3 *Mohammed Ali Jinnah's Speeches as Governor General of Pakistan 1947–48* (Karachi: Government of Pakistan, 1948).

4 Hussain Haqqani, *Pakistan Between Mosque and Military* (Pakistan: Vanguard Books, 2005), 16.

5 Ibid., 21–25.

6 Seyyed Vali Reza Nasr, *Mawdudi and the Making of Islamic Revivalism* (New York: Oxford University Press, 1996), 43.

7 Ibid.

8 Khalid B. Sayeed, *Politics in Pakistan: The Nature and Direction of Change* (New York: Praeger, 1980), 62.

9 Ziring, *Pakistan at the Cross-current of History*, 82.

10 Ian Talbot, *Pakistan: A Modern History* (Pakistan: Vanguard Books, 1999), 180–81.

11 Haqqani, *Pakistan Between Mosque and Military*, 54–55.

12 Ibid., 123–24.

13 Farzana Shaikh, *Making Sense of Pakistan* (London: Hurst, 2009), 95.

14 Ibid., 97.

15 Ibid.

16 Mushahid Hussain, "Changing Profile of Pakistani Army," *Frontier Post* (Pakistan), February 13, 1994.

17 Stephan Cohen, *The Pakistan Army* (Berkeley: University of California Press, 1988), 95.

18 Steve Cole, *Ghost Wars* (Harmondsworth, UK: Penguin, 2004), 63.

19 Mohammad Yousaf, *The Bear Trap: Afghanistan's Untold Story* (London: Leo Cooper, 1992), 113

20 Ayesha Jalal, *Democracy and Authoritarianism in South Asia* (Pakistan: Sang-E-Meel Publications, 1995), 109.

21 Ibid., 110.

22 southasia.oneworld.net/article/view/113823/1/.

23 www.washingtonpost.com/wp-dyn/content/article/2008/12/08/AR2008120803612.html; Zahid Hussain, *Frontline Pakistan*, 11.

24 news.bbc.co.uk/onthisday/hi/dates/stories/march/12/newsid_4272000/4272943.stm; spectator.org/archives/2005/05/11/derailing-d-company.

25 "Bhutto Clan Leaves Trail of Corruption," *New York Times*, January 9, 1998.

26 Hussain, *Frontline Pakistan*, 31.

27 Hassan Abbas, *Pakistan's Drift into Extremism* (New York: M. E. Sharpe, 2005), 169–75.

28 Ibid., 201.

29 Author interview with several Pakistan officers, 2009 to 2010.

30 Author interviews with senior Pakistani officials, 2009. Also see www
    .satp.org/satporgtp/kpsgill/2003/America.htm.
31 "Qaeda Suspect, Sound Asleep at Trail's End, Offers No Resistance,"
    New York Times, March 3, 2003.
32 georgewbush-whitehouse.archives.gov/news/ releases/2003/.

Chapter 3:

1   This description is based on a series of interviews with close aides of
    Musharraf and government officials. Also see "Dangerous Liaison,"
    Newsline, January 2004.
2   "Dangerous Liaison, *Newsline*, January 2004.
3   Musharraf, *In the Line of Fire*, 247.
4   "Pakistan Reports Arrest of a Senior al Qaeda Leader," *New York Times*,
    May 5, 2005.
5   Author interview with a senior army officer, 2005.
6   "Despite U.S. Efforts, Pakistan Remains Key Terror Hub," *Wall Street
    Journal*, July 22, 2005.
7   Al Jazeera, September 2003.
8   "The Taliban Strike Back," *Newsline*, September 2003.
9   Ibid.
10 "Tribal Tribulation: A Campaign to Flush Out Islamic Militants Hiding
    in Pakistan's Wild West Tests the Will of Islamabad and the U.S.," *Time*,
    May 17, 2004.
11 Author interview with President Hamid Karzai, December 2003. Also
    see Rashid, *Descent into Chaos*, 246.
12 Musharraf, *In the Line of Fire*, 265.
13 "Amid U.S. Policy Dispute, Qaeda Grows in Pakistan," *New York Times*,
    June 30, 2008.
14 *Dawn (Pakistan)*, March 16, 2004.
15 news.bbc.co.uk/2/hi/south_asia/8287714.stm; www.longwarjournal
    .org/archives/2009/10/tahir_yuldashev_conf.php.
16 Author interview with Abdullah Mehsud, 2003.
17 "All Quiet on Northwestern Front," *Newsline*, May 2004.
18 Ibid.
19 "Al Qaeda Finds Its Center of Gravity," *New York Times*, September 10,
    2006.
20 Author interview with local resident in Wana, 2004.
21 Musharraf, *In the Line of Fire*, 266.
22 "Defiant in Death," *Newsline*, August 2007.
23 www.washingtonpost.com/wp-dyn/articles/A52670–2004Oct21.html.

24 Interview with Abdullah Mehsud. BBC, 2004.

25 Ibid.

26 BBC News, July 24, 2007.

27 "Defiant in Death," *Newsline*, August 2007.

28 www.newsweek.com/2008/01/05/al-qaeda-s-newest-triggerman.html.

29 Ibid.

30 "Pakistan Paid Million to Surrender: Money Used to 'Repay' Al Qaeda's Debt," *Dawn (Pakistan)*, February 9, 2005. Also see www.newsweek .com/2008/01/05/al-qaeda-s-newest-triggerman.html.

31 www.dailytimes.com.pk/default.asp?page=story_8–2–2005_pg1_9.

32 Author interview with a senior government official, 2009. Also see "Baitullah Mehsud, Pakistan's Biggest Dilemma," *Dawn (Pakistan)*, December 31, 2007.

33 Press conference in Rawalpindi, 2006.

34 www.satp.org/satporgtp/countries/pakistan/Waziristan/timeline/ 2005.htm.

35 www.washingtonpost.com/wp-dyn/content/article/2005/05/14/ AR2005051401121.html.

36 Ibid.

37 Ibid.

38 www.washingtonpost.com/wp-dyn/content/article/2005/12/03/ AR2005120301473_pf.html.

39 www.dailytimes.com.pk/default.asp?page=2005%5C12%5C06%5C story_6–12–2005_pg1_3.

40 "Evidence Suggests U.S. Missiles Used in Strike," NBC News Service, December 5, 2005, www.msnbc.msn.com/id/10303175/.

41 news.bbc.co.uk/2/hi/south_asia/5096008.stm.

42 "Deadly Dilemma," *Newsline*, November 2006.

43 Ibid.

44 BBC News, September 2004, bbc.co.uk/2/hi/middle_east/1560834 .stm.

45 Author interview with a senior Pakistani security official, 2009.

46 "Air Strikes by U.S. Draw Protest from Pakistanis," *New York Times,* January 15, 2006.

47 Ibid.

48 Associated Press, January, 15, 2006.

49 www.worldwizzy.com/learn/index.php/Damadola_airstrike.

50 "Bush Said to Give Orders Allowing Raids in Pakistan," *New York Times*, September 11, 2008.

51 Ibid.

52 "Bush Offers Praise to Pakistani Leader," *Washington Post*, March 5, 2006.

Notes

53 "Taliban Tighten Grip in Northern Pakistan," *New York Times*, December 11, 2006.

54 Author interview with a senior retired army officer, 2009.

55 Zahid Hussain, "It's War Now," *Newsweek*, January 16, 2006.

56 "Amid U.S. Policy Disputes al Qaeda Grows in Pakistan," *New York Times*, June 30, 2008.

57 Ibid.

58 Rashid, *Descent into Chaos*, 277.

59 Zahid Hussain, "Deadly Dilemma," *Newsline*, November 2006.

60 Zahid Hussain, "Running out of Options," *Newsweek*, November 13, 2006.

61 Ibid.

62 "Deadly Dilemma," *Newsline*, November 2006.

63 Zahid Hussain, "Running out of Options, *Newsweek*, November 13, 2006.

64 Ibid.

65 "Suicide Bombing Kills 41 Troops at Pakistan Army Base," *Washington Post*, November 9, 2006.

66 www.washingtonpost.com/wp-dyn/content/article/2007/02/20/AR2007022001493.html.

67 Ibid.

68 "Rice put Musharraf Under Pressure to Rein In Taliban. *Guardian*, February 19, 2007.

Chapter 4:

1 "Taliban Militancy Could Engulf Pakistan," *New York Times*, June 29, 2007.

2 Ibid.

3 Zahid Hussain, "Terror in Miranshah," *Newsline*, April 2006.

4 Ibid.

5 Ibid.

6 Author interview with the official, 2007.

7 "Terror in Miranshah," *Newsline*, April 2006.

8 Rahimullah Yusufazai, "Eviction or Safe Passage," *Newsline*, May 2007.

9 Author interview with local residents, 2007.

10 Fazlullah, public address in Imamdehri in Swat, 2007.

11 Kamran Rehmat, "Swat: Pakistan's Lost Paradise," al Jazeera website, January 27, 2009.

12 Rageh Omar, "Battle for Pakistan's Soul," *New Statesman*, July 12, 2007.

Rageh, a reporter for al Jazeera, interviewed Abdul Rashid several times on a cell phone during the fighting.

13 *Dawn (Pakistan)*, July 9, 2007; *Post*, July 8, 2007.

14 Graham Ushar, "Red Mosque: Endgame for Musharraf?" *The Nation*, July 30, 2007.

15 *The Times (London)*, July 6, 2007; *Newsline*, August 2007.

16 Abdul Rashid, telephone interview with GEO, a private Pakistani TV channel.

17 "Pakistan Cleric Offers Surrender," BBC News website, July 5, 2007, http://news.bbc.co.uk/2/hi/south_asia/6274518.stm.

18 "Pakistani Colonel Killed in Clash," BBC News website, July 8, 2007, http://news.bbc.co.uk/2/hi/south_asia/6281404.stm.

19 I witnessed the conversation outside the Lal Masjid.

20 AFP, July 9, 2007.

21 Hamid Mir, *Jang* (Pakistani newspaper). He narrated the story to the author.

22 Ibid.

23 Author interviews with several members of Lal Masjid.

24 Abdullah's followers believed the cleric was assassinated by a radical Shia group.

25 Tariq Ismail Sagar, *Operation Silence*, (Pakistan: Tahir Sons Publishers, 2007).

26 Syed Saleem Shahzad, "The Taliban's Brothers in Alms," *Asia Times* website, March 14, 2007.

27 Author interview with a senior government official. Ejazul Haq also confirmed it in an interview with a Pakistani TV channel.

28 I met with Molly at the Lal Masjid in January 2007.

29 Author interview with a senior aide to Musharraf, 2007.

30 Osama bin Laden's statement was part of a twenty-three-minute video that was also posted on a radical Islamic website.

31 Zawahiri's statement was posted on a radical Islamic website.

32 Abdul Rashid Ghazi had issued the statement at the start of the siege of Lal Masjid.

33 *Pakistan Security Report 2008* (Islamabad: Pak Institute for Peace Studies, 2008).

34 Author interview with a senior Pakistani security official. Captain Khuram was killed fighting against the NATO forces in Afghanistan's Helmand province in 2007.

Notes

Chapter 5:

1 "Pakistan Rebels Display Hostages," BBC News, October 11, 2007, news.bbc.co.uk/2/hi/south_asia/7039101.stm.

2 "Pakistan's Most Wanted Warlord," *US News & World Report*, January 2008, http://politics.usnews.com/news/world/articles/2008/01/28/pakistans-most-wanted-warlord.html.

3 Benazir Bhutto, *Reconciliation* (New York: Simon & Schuster, 2008), 225.

4 Author interview with Musharraf, January 2007.

5 Author interview with Wajid Shamshul Hasan, Pakistan's high commissioner to the United Kingdom and a close aide to Benazir Bhutto, 2008.

6 Bhutto, *Reconciliation*.

7 www.whitehouse.gov/issues/homeland-security/.

8 Author interview with a senior Pakistani counterterrorism official, 2009.

9 "Taliban Ideologue Survives," *Daily Times (Pakistan)*, May 26, 2008.

10 www.dailytimes.com.pk/default.asp?page=2008%5C05%5C26%5Cstory_26–5–2008_pg7_2.

11 Author interview with the boy and his father in Mingora, Swat, June 2009.

12 Author interview in Mingora, July 2009.

13 Author interview with residents of Mingora, April 2009.

14 www.criticalthreats.org/pakistan/survivalist-north-waziristan-hafiz-gul-bahadur-biography-and-analysis.

15 Ron Suskind, *The Way of the World* (New York: Harper and Row, 2008), 262–65.

16 Ibid.

17 Ibid.

18 Ibid.

19 Author interview, an aide of Benazir Bhutto, 2009.

20 Interview with Benazir Bhutto, *Newsweek*, December 15, 2007.

21 Bhutto, *Reconciliation*, 221–22

22 www.skynewstranscripts.co.uk/transcript.asp?id=387.

23 http://www.guardian.co/uk/world/2007/oct/19/pakistan.benazirbhutto2.

24 www.skynewstranscripts.co.uk/transcript.asp?id=387.

25 *Dawn (Pakistan)*, November 7, 2007.

26 Interview with Benazir Bhutto, MSNBC, November 3, 2007, msnbc.msn.com/id/21612806/.

27 Musharraf confirmed the report in a meeting in London in June 2009.

28 Zahhid Hussain, *Frontline Pakistan*, xvi.

29 UN Commission report, released April 15, 2010, un.org/apps/news/story.asp?NewsID=34384&Cr=bhutto&Cr1.

Chapter 6:

1 Author interviews with close friends of and aides to Benazir Bhutto, 2009.

2 Ibid.

3 Author interview with Gen. Mahmood Ali Durrani, 2008.

4 "Switzerland Frees $60 Million Zardari Assets," *New York Times*, August 27, 2008.

5 "Bush Said to Give Orders Allowing Raids in Pakistan," *New York Times*, September 11, 2008.

6 www.newsweek.com/2008/09/12/pakistan-s-dangerous-double-game.html.

7 Author interview with a senior Pakistani diplomat, 2010.

8 "Abu Laith al-Libbi," *Washington Post*, February 1, 2008.

9 "Death from Above: How Predator Is Taking Its Toll on al Qaeda," *The Times (London)*, January 3, 2009.

10 "CIA Expands Use of Drones in Pakistan," *New York Times*, December 3, 2009.

11 "Usama al-Kini, Head of al Qaeda in Pakistan, Killed by U.S. Military," *The Times (London)*, January 9, 2009.

12 "U.S. Missile Strikes Said to Take Heavy Toll on al Qaeda," *Los Angeles Times*, March 22, 2009.

13 www.brookings.edu/ . . . /2009/0714_targeted_killings_byman.aspx.

14 "UN Envoy Seeks More U.S. Openness on War Deaths," Reuters, June, 3, 2009.

15 "UN Envoy Slams U.S. for Unanswered Drone Questions," Reuters, October 27, 2009.

16 "CIA Expands Use of Drones in Pakistan," *New York Times*, December 3, 2009.

17 www.pid.gov.pk/press22-07-09.htm.

18 "U.S. Military, Pak Carrying Out Predator Drone Missions Together," *Los Angeles Times*, May 13, 2009.

19 Jan Mayer, "The Predator War," *New Yorker*, October 26, 2009.

20 Author interview with a senior government official in North West Frontier Province, 2009.

21 According to military.

22 "Zardari Details Swat Peace Term," BBC News, February 17, 2009, news.bbc.co.uk/1/hi/world/south_asia/7894581.stm.

23 Author interview with a senior security officer in the region, 2009.

24 "Taliban Move Closer to Islamabad," Wall Street Journal, April 23, 2009.

25 Ibid.

26 Author interview with Nawaz Sharif, 2009.

27 Ibid.

28 Author interview with an officer in Mingora, 2009.

29 Ibid.

Chapter 7:

1 "Accused Terror Scientist in Court," The Times (London), August 7, 2008.

2 "Family Affairs, Just Maybe, at Courthouse," New York Times, December 8, 2009.

3 A group of gunmen attacked a bus carrying the Sri Lankan cricket team in a busy commercial area in Lahore, killing six people. "Gunmen Shoot Sri Lankan Cricketers," BBC News, March 3, 2009.

4 "Pakistan Vows to Take Revenge for the Attack by Taliban," Wall Street Journal, October 12, 2009.

5 Author interview with Gen. Athar Abbas, chief military spokesman, 2009.

6 Author interview with a senior Pakistani intelligence official, 2009.

7 News International (Pakistan), September 2008.

8 Author interview with a senior Pakistani intelligence official, 2009.

9 "Al Qaeda Family: Al Qaeda Attacks," CBC News, March 3, 2004, www.cbc.ca/news/background/khadr/alqaedafamily5.html.

10 Dawn (Pakistan), May 13, 2009.

11 Author interview with a senior investigative officer, 2010.

12 "Militant Held Who Led the Attack on Army Base," The Times (London), October 12, 2009; "Pakistan Vows to Take Revenge," Wall Street Journal, October 12, 2009.

13 Author interview with Maj. Gen. Athar Abbas, 2009.

14 afpak.foreignpolicy.com/posts/2010/04/30/the_new_new_face_of_the_pakistani_taliban.

15 "U.S. Resumes Surveillance Flight over Pakistan," New York Times, June 29, 2009.

16 Author interview with General Abbas, 2009.

17 Author interview with a military officer in Waziristan, November 2009.

18 Author interview with a senior army officer in Sararogha, November 2009.

19 "Army Discovers Trail of Top 9/11 Suspect," *The Times (London)*, October 30, 2009.

20 Author interview with Lt. Gen. Athar Abbas, 2009.

21 Author interview with a survivor, 2010.

22 "U.S. Military Says Its Forces Are Insufficient in Afghanistan," *Wall Street Journal*, August 23, 2009.

23 "Pakistan Vows to Revenge Taliban Assault," *Wall Street Journal*, October 12, 2009.

24 "Pakistan's Dangerous Double Game," *Newsweek*, September 13, 2008.

25 "Aid Package from U.S. Jolts Its Army in Pakistan," *New York Times*, October 7, 2009.

26 Author interview with a senior Pakistani Army officer, 2010.

27 "U.S. Military Hardware Not Reserved for Pakistan, said Garry Akerman, Head of House Foreign Affairs Subcommittee on Middle East and South Asia," *Dawn (Pakistan)*, June 12, 2010.

28 News International (Pakistan), October 15, 2009.

29 *Los Angeles Times*, October 31, 2009.

30 *The Nation (Pakistan)*, October 31, 2009.

31 Author interview with a senior Pakistani diplomat, 2010.

32 Author interview with a senior Pakistani official, 2010.

33 "U.S. Plans New Drone Attacks in Pakistan," *Wall Street Journal*, March 26, 2009.

34 Author interview with Lt. Gen. Athar Abbas, May 2010.

35 Author interview with a Pakistani official, 2010.

36 Author interview with a senior military officer, May 2010.

37 http://www.surgeusa.org/global/westpoint.htm.

38 "CIA to Expand Use of Drones in Pakistan," *New York Times*, December 3, 2009.

Chapter 8:

1 www.cbsnews.com/stories/2010/01/06/world/main6060902.shtml.

2 http://www.washingtonpost.com/wp-dyn/content/article/2010/03/17/AR2010031702558.html.

3 "Pakistani Taliban Are Said to Expand Alliance," *New York Times*, May 7, 2010.

4 "U.S. Drone Strike Targets Pakistan Taliban Chief Hakimullah Mehsud," *Daily Telegraph*, January 14, 2010.

5 http://www.washingtonpost.com/wp-dyn/content/article/2010/03/17/AR2010031702558.html.

6 www.state.gov/secretary/rm/2010/07/144827.htm.

Notes

7 "For the Times Sq. Suspect Long Roots of Discontent," *New York Times,* May 15, 2010.

8 Ibid.

9 "Faisal Shahzad: 'Modern Boy' from Liberal Pakistani Village," *Daily Dawn (Pakistan),* May 5, 2010, http://www.dawn.com/wps/wcm/connect/dawn-content-library/dawn/news/pakistan/04-faisal-shahzad-profile-qs-06.

10 "Caterer Arrested in New York Plot," *Wall Street Journal,* May 21, 2010.

11 "Students Linked to al Qaeda," *Wall Street Journal,* December 11, 2009.

12 http://www.ft.com/cms/s/0/464c894c-7faf-11df-91b4-00144feabdc0.html.

13 www.longwarjournal.org/threat-matrix/archives/2010/05/times_square_bomber_met_with_q.php.

14 http://www.reuters.com/article/idUSTRE65K68420100621.

15 According to a senior Pakistani diplomat.

16 http://www.reuters.com/article/idUSTRE6445DM20100507.

17 "U.S Presses Pakistan for More Data on Traveling," *New York Times,* May 30, 2010.

18 Ibid.

19 news.bbc.co.uk/2/hi/americas/8669512.stm.

20 Author interview with a senior Pakistani official, 2010.

21 "The Marines Move on Marja: A Perilous Slog Against Afghanistan's Taliban," *Washington Post,* February 15, 2010.

22 AFP: May 26, 2010.

23 "Taliban Hold Sway in Area Taken by U.S.," *New York Times,* May 17, 2010.

24 afghanistan.blogs.cnn.com/2010/05/06/losing-hearts-and-minds-in-marjah/.

25 Maleeha Lodhi, "Perils of Obama's Afghan Policy," *The News,* December 7, 2009.

26 www.newsweek.com/2010/03/18/the-gang-that-couldn-t-shoot-straight.html.

27 "U.S. Approves Training to Expand Afghan Army," *New York Times,* January 15, 2010.

28 "Drug Use, Poor Discipline Afflict Afghanistan's Army," *Wall Street Journal,* July 28, 2010.

29 Ibid.

30 Author interview with a senior Pakistani security official, 2009.

31 Interview with Maj. Gen. Athar Abbas, 2010.

32 General Kayani, briefing to a group of journalists, February 2010.

33 "Karzai Is Said to Doubt West Can Defeat Taliban," *New York Times,* June 11, 2010.

34 Ibid.
35 www.uspolicyinabigworld.com/2010/06/20/isi-taliban-collusion/.
36 "U.S. Wrestling with Olive Branch for Taliban," *New York Times*, January 27, 2010.
37 Ibid.
38 "17 Die in Kabul Bomb Attack," *New York Times*, October 9, 2009.
39 Ibid.
40 http://www.washingtonpost.com/wp-dyn/content/article/2010/06/06/AR2010060600714.html.
41 Interview with Maj. General Athar Abbas, 2010.
42 "Pakistan's Push on Afghan Peace Leaves U.S. Wary," *New York Times*, June 28, 2010.
43 Ibid.
44 www.nytimes.com/2010/07/27/world/asia/27wikileaks.html?ref=wikileaks.

Acknowledgments

I am extremely grateful to all my colleagues and friends who have helped and supported me in the process of writing this book. I owe thanks hugely to Rehana Hakim and Samina Ibrahim at *Newsline*, with whom I share more than twenty-seven years of my career as a journalist.

My especial thanks to Farah Durrani, who motivated me to write this book, and to Zeeshan Afzal Khan, Kathy Gannon, Carol Grisanti, and Francoise Chipaux for their invaluable support.

Maleeha Lodhi has been a great source of intellectual inspiration. I am particularly grateful to Zeba Satthar for her invaluable suggestions, which helped me a great deal.

I owe a great deal to both my editor at Free Press, Emily Loose, and my agent, Jessica Woollard. Emily with her highly skillful editing and hard work made it possible to bring this book out so quickly.

Index

Index

Index

Index

Index

military, U.S.:
  Afghanistan deployment of, 11,
    26, 156, 185
  along Afghanistan-Pakistan
    border, 15–16
  al Qaeda hunted by, 34, 146
  Haqqani network targeted by, 38
  militant attacks on, 1, 2, 3, 4, 34,
    60, 65, 66, 67, 68, 72, 85, 87
  in Pakistani military operations,
    33, 37, 84, 194, 195–96
  Pakistani raids by, 146
  Tora Bora offensive by, 26, 27
Mingora, Pakistan, 160–61
Minni, Ahmed, 192–93
Miranshah, Pakistan, Taliban rule
  over, 95–96
Misri, Abu al-Obaida al-, 89
Mohammad, Atta, 65
Mohammed, Faqir, 82, 135, 154
Mohammed, Khalid Sheikh, 28, 61,
  64, 165
Mohammed, Malwi Faqir, 95
Mohammed, Maulana Sufi, 99–100,
  151, 156
Mohammed, Nek, 69, 71–72,
  73–74
Mohaqqiq, Ustad, 65
Mohmand, 95, 98, 142
Morrell, Geoff, 206
Mughul, Shoib, 192
Mujahideen, 4, 17, 18, 19–20, 21, 22,
  36, 55, 66, 208
Mullen, Mike, 146
Mursi, Midhat, 147
Musharraf, Pervez:
  assassination attempts on, 63–64,
    80, 113, 170
  Benazir Bhutto's relations with,
    125–29, 137, 138, 139, 141
  coup by, 60
  drone attacks defended by, 88, 90

  Kashmir militancy support
    denied by, 25
  in Lal Masjid conflict, 110, 111,
    116
  militancy policies of, 5, 27–29,
    32, 33, 34, 38, 39, 42, 60–62,
    65, 66, 67, 68, 72, 78, 79,
    83–84, 85, 86, 87, 89, 90–91,
    94, 103, 130
  military command renounced
    by, 140
  as military leader, 59, 127
  opposition to, 25, 30, 61, 70, 71,
    86, 103–5, 106, 113, 125, 126,
    128, 130–31, 140
  resignation of, 144, 210
  Sharif's return opposed by, 140
  state of emergency declared by,
    130, 139, 140
  U.S. alliance with, 25, 26–28, 30,
    31, 33, 39, 61, 64–65, 66, 67,
    74, 85, 86, 90–91, 103, 113,
    118, 126, 130, 140, 144
  U.S. criticized by, 67, 74
Muslim Americans, in al Qaeda, 8
Muslim Brotherhood, 36
Muslim League, 43
Muttehida Majlis Amal (MMA), 29,
  60, 95, 98

Nasir, Javed, 58
National Reconciliation Ordinance,
  129
NATO forces:
  in Afghanistan, 11, 67, 131, 153,
    175, 196–97, 210
  militant attacks on, 2, 3, 4, 87,
    136
Nazir, Malwi, 97, 135, 156, 175
Negroponte, John, 139
Netherlands, 210
Niwani, Rashid Akbar, 134

Index

About the Author

Zahid Hussain is an award-winning journalist and writer, a senior editor with *Newsline*, and a correspondent for *The Times of London*, *The Wall Street Journal*, and *Newsweek*. He has also covered Pakistan and Afghanistan for several other international publications, including the Associated Press and *The Economist*. He appears regularly on BBC World Service and CNN. His book *Frontline Pakistan: The Struggle with Militant Islam* has won widespread acclaim as a seminal text on the subject. He lives in Pakistan.